With sound magickal advice, heartfelt
knowledge, and humor, Deborah Blake has
crafted an entertaining guide for any season.
—*Raven Digitalis*, author of *Goth Craft*
and *Shadow Magick Compendium*

This handy book helps sort through all the
noise and presents practical, fun ways to live
"La Vida Wicca" in all aspects of your life.
—*Gail Wood*, author of
Rituals of the Dark Moon

An Amusing,
Inspiring & Informative
Guide to the
Wonderful World
of Witchcraft

Photo: John Mazarak

ABOUT THE AUTHOR

Deborah Blake is a Wiccan high priestess who has been leading an eclectic group, Blue Moon Circle, since Beltane 2004. She is the author of *Circle, Coven & Grove: A Year of Magickal Practice*, published by Llewellyn in 2007, and has written a number of articles for Pagan publications, including *Llewellyn's 2008 Witches' Companion*.

Deborah was also a finalist in the Pagan Fiction Award Contest, and her short story, "Dead and (Mostly) Gone," is included in *The Pagan Anthology of Short Fiction: 13 Prize-Winning Tales*. She is currently working on her third book for Llewellyn, as well as a novel featuring, naturally, a Witch.

When not writing, Deborah manages the Artisans' Guild, a cooperative shop she founded with a friend in 1999, and works as a jewelry maker, tarot reader, ordained minister, and intuitive energy healer. She lives in a 100-year-old farmhouse in rural upstate New York with five cats who supervise all her activities, both magickal and mundane.

Deborah Blake

Everyday Witch A to Z

An
Amusing, Inspiring
& Informative Guide to the
Wonderful World of Witchcraft

Llewellyn Publications
Woodbury, Minnesota

FIRST EDITION
First Printing, 2008

Book design and editing by Rebecca Zins
Cover design by Lisa Novak
Cover image: John Rawsterne/iStockphoto

Cover cat(s) used for illustrative purposes only
and may not endorse or represent the book's subject

Llewellyn is a registered trademark of Llewellyn Worldwide, Ltd.

Library of Congress Cataloging-in-Publication Data

Blake, Deborah, 1960-
Everyday witch A to Z : an amusing, inspiring & informative guide to
the wonderful world of witchcraft / Deborah Blake.—1st ed.
    p. cm.
Includes bibliographical references.
ISBN 978-0-7387-1275-8
1. Witchcraft—Miscellanea. I. Title.
BF1566.B5345 2008
133.4´303—dc22

2008026593

Llewellyn Publications
A Division of Llewellyn Worldwide, Ltd.
2143 Wooddale Drive, Dept. 0-7387-1275-8
Woodbury, MN 55125-2989
www.llewellyn.com

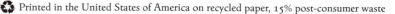 Printed in the United States of America on recycled paper, 15% post-consumer waste

Dedication

As always, this book is dedicated to my two families—

My magickal family, Blue Moon Circle, without whom none of this would exist. You make my life a better place, and every moment we spend together is a gift from the gods (who clearly have a strange sense of humor). Thanks for always loving everything I write, no matter what. Special thanks to Robin, for help above and beyond the call of duty with the last-minute frantic research, maintaining the Blue Moon website, and all that other clever stuff.

My "muggle" family, the Levines, the Conleys, the Constantines (not to mention the Neisulers and the Rothmans)—thanks for always being so supportive of my efforts and my nontraditional life. You are all pretty magickal too! (And you hardly ever made me sleep in that cupboard under the stairs...)

This book is especially dedicated to the next generation:

My little Witches Shaylee Dawn, Sophia Gaea, and our newest addition, Nathaniel—I was there when you came into this turn of the cycle, and I can't wait to watch you grow and blossom.

And the Conley/Constantine bunch: Brianna, Addison, Athena, and Stamo—Athena may be the only one named after a goddess, but you are all beautiful (or handsome), smart, creative, and very, very cool. And I'm not just saying that because I'm your aunt. I know you're all going to do great things.

With immense gratitude, as always, to the gang at Llewellyn: Elysia, who took a good book and encouraged me (well, kicked my butt) until I made it a great one; Jen, who does her best to make me famous; and Becky, who made this book even better than I could ever have imagined. You all ROCK!

And in memory of Tony: your heart was true and everlasting, the drum rang out beneath your hands, your circle family mourned your passing but know you play on in the Summerlands. Blessed be.

Table of Contents

Introduction

I wrote this book for you. Yes, that's right: you.

If you are new to Witchcraft and searching for knowledge, this book was written for you.

If you have been walking the path for many years and need something fun to remind you of what drew you to the Craft, this book was written for you.

If you are curious about Witches or simply interested in exploring the ideas and beliefs of the Pagan world, this book was written for you.

And if you have ever felt the touch of something enchanted in the woods or heard the goddess's whisper in the sound of the waves on the shore, this book is for you.

I wrote this book for anyone who is or might be a Witch. Is that you?

Inside these pages, you will find the serious and the silly, the factual and the fanciful, the irreverent and the inspirational. In short, you will find a little sampling of all those things that make up the everyday Witch.

For while we may don our cloaks and robes for special occasions and gather under the night sky when the moon is full, the truth is that we are Witches all day, every day. Our beliefs, our spiritual practices, and our relationships to each other define who we are as we walk through our everyday lives.

It is my hope that the contents of this book will educate, entertain, and inspire you, and bring a touch of the magickal to your everyday life. And if it makes you laugh out loud a few times, that's good too.

Because living the life of a Witch isn't just a matter of serious beliefs and heartfelt worship—it is also full of fun and joy and laughter.

So open up to any page and find something that will make you think or dream or laugh—or maybe all three at once, because it is that kind of book!

—Deborah Blake (Onyx)

Magic the Cat's Introduction

Now, me? I just wrote it for the catnip. Seriously. My Witch, Onyx (you might know her as Deborah Blake), promised me a whole bunch of catnip if I would help her write this book. Not that she really needed my help, of course. She's a very good Witch and a pretty good writer on her own. But as any of you who have animals know, your furry friends can always add a little something special to whatever you do.

So I told her I would give her a paw. I've included some of my simple spells and herbal helpers (cats know a lot about herbs—like which ones to eat and which ones just to knock on the floor—so you can trust me on this) and a few words of wisdom to my fellow familiars that I thought might be useful.

I helped organize the book, too. Starting with A and ending with Z? My idea. But inside each letter, you won't find things in such strict order. After all, us magickal types don't like to follow the rules all the time. That would just be boring. And it seemed only right to start a book on Witchcraft with "Attitude"!

But mostly I just supervised, as usual. Sat on her lap while she typed and gave her a subtle hint or two when something wasn't as funny or as informative as she thought it was. (It's amazing how a sharp nip on the ear can focus the mind.) So if you like the book, I will take all the credit. Of course, any complaints can be addressed to her...

So pull up a chair, grab a furry pal if you're lucky enough to have one, and start reading. Oh, and if there's any catnip in the pages, it's mine!

Familiarly,

—Magic the Cat

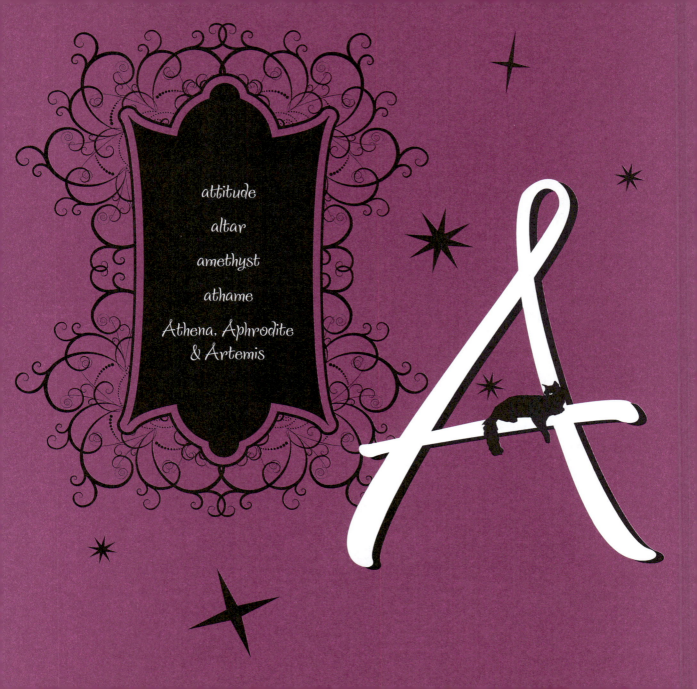

attitude

altar

amethyst

athame

Athena, Aphrodite
& Artemis

Attitude

If you're a Witch, you've probably got attitude. If you don't, I'll bet your witchy friends will help you find some.

Attitude is that little extra bounce in your walk because you are getting a zing from nature, whether it is the shine from the full moon, the call of the coyote up on the hill, or the crash of the waves on the shore.

Attitude is your secret smile that says that you know a few things that most of the folks around you don't.

Attitude is having a charm in your pocket, a chant on your lips, and faith in your heart.

Attitude is being a Witch—and proud of it.

So smile that smile, sweet Witch, and make the most of who and what you are—but don't forget to stay just a bit humble...after all, the gods are watching, and there is such a thing as too much attitude!

Altar

They say that home is where the heart is—if so, then a Witch's home is her altar. That is where your most precious tools live: athame, god and goddess candles, incense, crystals...whatever you use to connect with the gods in your most private rituals.

Your altar is where you go when you are most troubled and in need of help. It is where you go in your greatest moments of joy to give thanks.

You stand at your altar to summon what you want and banish what you don't, to ask for help and to ask for answers.

What better definition of home could you have?

So tend your altar carefully. Find items that you will treasure, and set them lovingly in their places. You don't need a lot. One candle or six (god and goddess and the four quarters)—it's your choice. That one perfect leaf, feather, or rock. As long as it means something to you, your altar is where it belongs.

And your altar is where you belong, too. It is the one place where you can truly be you, with nothing hidden or held back. Laugh, cry, howl, or simply be silent…it's all good.

So go to your altar often, even if only for a minute or two at a time, and check in with yourself, the gods, and the universe. Ground back to the earth and to your truest self. And don't forget to dust on occasion, either.

Helpful Hints:
"Hidden in Plain Sight: Altar Alternatives"

Most Witches like to have an altar, but not every Witch lives someplace where he or she is comfortable having all that magickal stuff right out in plain view. So here is a list of the usual items we witchy types tend to have on our altars, and a few possible, less obviously Pagan substitutes:

GOD/GODDESS STATUES = GOLD/SILVER CANDLES OR PLAQUE OF
    THE TREE OF LIFE

ATHAME = FANCY LETTER-OPENER OR WOODEN BRANCH

CHALICE = ANY NICE CUP OR GOBLET, OR SMALL BOWL

SALT & WATER = STONE AND SEASHELL

QUARTER CANDLES = ROCK (EARTH), FEATHER (AIR), SHELL (WATER),
    AND TEALIGHT (FIRE)

You can always put out flowers as an offering and a few colored stones (for the quarters), and no one will be the wiser. After all, you know what they're for—and so do the gods—and that's all that really matters.

AMETHYST

If you're only going to have one stone to use with your magickal work, get an amethyst. Amethyst is one of the best all-around gemstones there is, and its use as a magickal tool is as old as time.

Gemstones in general are perfect for use in magick because they come from the ground, gifts of Mother Earth and full of her power and energy. Amethyst in particular is an especially powerful stone and is good for a multitude of magickal tasks. One of its common uses is for love magick, either to draw it in or to aid in keeping the love you already have.

Amethyst can also be used to boost courage, promote peace or prophetic dreams, overcome addictions, increase psychic ability, and help you sleep. Amethyst is a powerful protective stone, said to shield its wearer from illness, harm, and any type of danger.

Most of all, amethyst is a healing stone, probably at least in part because it is good for calming the stressed-out mind and spirit. (Not that any of us ever have problems with that!)

And last but not least, amethyst is beautiful, the deep purple of the desert at dusk or of a goddess's eyes.

So get a crystal, a chunk, or a globe of amethyst, and put it on your altar or around your neck. Then go work some magick!

Magic the Cat's Simple Spells:
"Amethyst Dreams"

To dream about love, put a few drops of rose essential oil on a piece of amethyst, and place it under your pillow. (Use a small piece, or you'll never get to sleep!)

Want to be a Witch on the cutting edge? Then you need to have at least one knife, maybe two. The athame (ATH-ah-may) is one tool that almost all Witches end up getting eventually. A double-edged straight knife that is used for pointing and directing energy during ritual, the athame can be made out of any material and decorated a little or a lot, depending on your preference.

The athame represents masculine energy or the god (probably because it is long, hard, and pointy—Pagans are not so big on the subtle, in case you haven't noticed yet). Some traditions connect it to the element of air and use it as a symbol of intellect, while others consider it a symbol of the element of fire. Use it for whichever seems right to you. Either way, the athame is not used for actual cutting but rather to trace signs of invoking or banishing, to project energy as an extension of your will, to inscribe the circle during casting, or simply to mix salt and water.

If you want to make a store-bought athame your own, you can add decorations such as feathers, runes, or the like (some knives have wooden handles, into which you can carve symbols or your Witch name, should you so choose).

Some Witches believe that you should never buy your own athame (or, for that matter, that all your tools should be either found or given to you as gifts), but that isn't always practical. They also say that if you are given a knife, you need to pay the person a penny or the gift will cut the friendship. I don't know if that's true, but why risk it? More importantly, if you are not sure where your athame was before it got to you, be sure to cleanse and consecrate it before you use it for powerful (or even not-so-powerful) magick. Nobody likes a magickal tool with cooties.

You might also want to get a boline, which is a curved knife, usually with a white handle, that can be used for harvesting herbs, cutting cords, or any other practical magickal task for which the athame is not suitable. The boline (or bolline) is a nice extra, but an athame is a must-have tool for most Witches. Just don't try to pack it in your carry-on luggage...

Helpful Hints:
"Call of Nine, My Athame Is Fine"

I found this rhyme to call power into an athame before casting a spell in Raven
Grimassi's terrific book *Encyclopedia of Wicca & Witchcraft*:[1]

Raise the blade into the air and say the following words:

Gracious goddess

Holy and divine

Answer to the call of nine.

One—I stand before thy throne

Two—I invoke thee alone

Three—I hold aloft my blade

Four—descend as the spell is made

Five—lend thy power to give it life

Six—thy power into my knife

Seven—on earth, in sky, and shining sea,

Gracious goddess, be with me

Eight—come now, the call is made

Nine—give power unto my blade.

---

1   Page 55.

10.   So they'll go with any color of robe.

9.   So you can cover up nicks and scratches with shoe polish.

8.   It's slimming. (Can't have fat athames, can we?)

7.   It doesn't show dirt.

6.   Because finding a dropped athame in an outdoor ritual in the dark is a test of loyalty to your faith.

5.   It's so much more dignified than chartreuse.

4.   Seemed like a good idea at the time.

3.   Someone spilled all the paints together, and that's what ended up.

2.   No, no! Black is for winter rituals—use *white* before Labor Day!

1.   So that we'd have something to argue about other than how *athame* is pronounced!

Ask Magic the Cat:
"Aura You a Good Witch?"

Dear Magic,

   My Witch says that she can see people's auras, and that she knows things about them from the way their auras look. What's an aura—and will she be able to tell I've been up on the counter again from looking at mine?

   Auristocat in Albany

Dear Auristocat,

   The aura is the energy field that surrounds all living things. It exists on three levels: the physical, the emotional, and the spiritual. Some people are able to perceive the auras of others on one or more of these levels. Your Witch may be picking up on physical auras (she can see if someone is sick) or on emotional auras (if someone is happy or sad). But don't worry—as far as I know, there's no such thing as an "I've been on the counter" aura, so I think you're okay. (But to be on the safe side, you may want to sit on top of the TV to block the vibes...)

   Familiarly,
   Magic the Cat

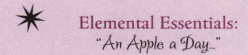

Elemental Essentials:
"An Apple a Day..."

Apples are a truly magickal fruit. If you cut one in half across the middle, you will see that they have a pentacle inside! Apple blossoms and apple wood are used for love and healing magick, and apple wood makes a great wand. It can also be burned on the fires at Samhain, since the apple is one of the symbols of that particular holiday. And of course, apple cider is the perfect drink for cakes and ale if you want something nonalcoholic in your chalice.

ATHENA, APHRODITE & ARTEMIS

Athena and Aphrodite and Artemis, oh my!

Many Witches call upon gods and goddesses from the Greek pantheon, and among my favorites are Athena, Aphrodite, and Artemis. These three powerful ladies were worshipped in Greece and the surrounding area right up until the advent of Christianity.

Athena is the counterpart of the Roman Minerva, and both were goddesses of war and wisdom (gee—you'd think that the two would be mutually exclusive, wouldn't you?). Unlike most of the (rather unruly) Greek gods, Athena was known for her discipline, as well as her gift to man of the olive tree, which was sacred to her. So whenever you have a martini, be sure to send thanks to this lovely lady. She was also the patron goddess of domestic crafts and shipbuilding.

Aphrodite is the goddess of sexual love and has connections to Ishtar, Astarte, and her Roman counterpart, Venus. She is said to have had a girdle with magickal properties—very handy for when the diet fails. (Oh, wait; I think that back then, *girdle* just meant "belt.") Her sacred animal was the goat, so if you are making an offering to her, why not try some goat's milk cheese?

Artemis is known as the huntress and is a goddess of animals and hunting, as well as being a maiden goddess. She was often shown with wings, surrounded by animals. This is one strong lady who stands for independence, self-esteem, and aggressiveness. The original feminist, if you will. She is a protector of women and is often called upon during labor.

Artemis is also the patron goddess of dogs (and a good one to invoke for any magick you might be doing for your pets). Here's an interesting tidbit I found in Yasmine Galenorn's book *Embracing the Moon*: "The word 'bitch' comes from Her, and was originally a positive term ('son of a bitch' literally meant 'son of the goddess')."[2] So the next time someone calls you a bitch, just smile and say thank you!

---

2 Page 245.

Witch 101:
"Amulets, Talismans, and Charms"

These three items are very useful witchy tools, but what are they, and how do you use them? And what the heck is the difference between an amulet, a talisman, and a charm, anyway?

I confess that I use the three terms more or less interchangeably, although according to Raymond Buckland, a talisman is human-made, whereas an amulet is natural (such as a bear claw, a stone with a hole worn into it, and so on).[3] Charms can be either of those or a charm bag, which is usually filled with herbs, along with perhaps a stone or other meaningful additions. Charms are either worn, carried, or used to protect a home or a tomb (if you should happen to have one of those that needs protecting).

The best description of these items and their use comes from *The Encyclopedia of Witches and Witchcraft*, which says they are "objects imbued with magical properties that protect against bad luck, illness and evil. Amulets are universal answers to age-old needs: to be healthy; to be virile and fertile; to be powerful and successful; to have good fortune."[4]

Generally, amulets with inscriptions are called charms, but otherwise I see no particular difference. And, hey, who cares what you call it as long as it works?

---

3 Buckland, *Buckland's Complete Book*, 255.
4 Guiley, *The Encyclopedia of Witches*, 8.

broomsticks

books

Beltane

banishing

Burning Times

B

BROOMSTICKS

Brooms aren't just for sweeping—at least not in the way that most people think.

Witches use brooms to clear away negativity from a room (spring cleaning, anyone?) or a ritual circle.

Brooms are also a symbol of Witches and Witchcraft that have been in use for centuries. They represent the freedom of flying (alas, only in our minds and spirits for most of us, unless we're Harry Potter) and the comfort of hearth and home.

A Witch's broom should never be used for everyday cleaning, but feel free to keep another broom for that—they are a handy household tool. As with your other tools, a ritual broom should be carefully tended and only used for magickal purposes.

One way to keep a special broom if you're still "in the broom closet" is to craft one out of broom straw, aromatic herbs, and colorful foliage (topped off with a spritz of glycerin to make it last), and hang it on your wall in full sight. After all, no one but you needs to know it is anything other than a clever, crafty decoration. (If you're craft-impaired, you can also just buy a pre-decorated broom and hang it up. I'll never tell.)

Helpful Hints:
"Spiritual Spring Cleaning"

For an easy way to spring-clean the energy in your home, consecrate a bowl of salt and water, then dip your magickal broom (not your everyday one) in the water and flick it around the corners and entrances to each room. While you're doing this, don't forget to visualize all the negativity being swept away!

A Book of Shadows is often a Witch's most prized possession. (Well, unless said Witch happens to own a Masarati ...)

It contains a Witch's rituals and spells (whether you write them yourself or copy them out of other sources) and anything else you need to keep track of your magickal work: correspondence lists that tell which candle colors to use for which spells, nifty herbal remedies, bits of poetry, and anything else that catches the eye, gladdens the heart, or lightens the spirit.

It is easy to make your own Book of Shadows. You can start from scratch by taking any blank book, notebook, or loose-leaf binder and decorating the cover with something witchy and cool. Or you can buy a premade book that says "Book of Shadows" right on the cover (in case anyone had any doubts about you being a Witch). If you are part of a coven, making a group Book of Shadows is a fun and moving activity, and it will help you keep track of all the fabulous things you do together. My group's BOS even has pictures of trips that we have taken together, along with rituals, spells, and "need to know" information.

In the good-old, bad-old days, a Witch's Book of Shadows was kept hidden and secret (to prevent both it and its owner from being burned). And if you live with mundanes or sticky-fingered children bearing crayons, you may still want to keep yours tucked away when it is not in use.

But please *do* share the treasures inside with others who believe as you do. Remember that the other purpose of a Book of Shadows is to hand all that carefully gathered information on to the next generation of Witches!

And while we're sharing books, let's not forget all those other books that can be sources for wonderful facts, fancy, and faith—Wicca how-tos and history, spirituality (ours and theirs), herbal lore, cookbooks, and even fiction.

My motto? You can't have too many books! (And don't forget to give a copy of this one to all your friends.)

BELTANE

Beltane is one of my favorite Pagan holidays. Unlike many of the more solemn rituals for which we gather, Beltane is lighthearted and downright bawdy. (Sorry kiddies, but this is *not* a G-rated holiday—at least not the way most of the folks I know celebrate it.)

Beltane, also spelled Beltaine, falls on May 1 and is often observed starting on May Eve at sundown on the night before. (That's right, we're talking about a twenty-four-hour party...I suggest you rest up!) It is a celebration of the marriage of the beautiful maiden goddess and the young god in his virile prime. I think you see where I'm going with this...

Traditionally, Beltane was a fertility holiday, and the day was used to bless the newly plowed fields and spread the seed for that year's crops. And people planted things, too.

In its most primitive form (before the spoil-sports got their hands on it), villages would select a young woman to be Queen of the May and a young man to be her consort for the day. Their joining was symbolic of the joining of the goddess and the god and would guarantee a good crop for that year.

This was a day on which everyone was issued a metaphorical "get out of jail free" card and invited to join in the celebration of spring, fertility, and the sun. Lots of babies were born nine months later, and to be a "Beltane baby" was considered good luck. (You know *somebody* got lucky.)

These days, we may not take the fertility element of the festivities quite so literally, but we still celebrate the joy and release that comes from the arrival of spring after a long, cold winter. Many Pagan gatherings still feature the traditional Maypole dance, which embodies the joyous and most bawdy aspects of the holiday.

Here's how you do it: The men all go off into the woods and cut down a tree (one that's already dead), then trim it until it is a long pole. The women dig a hole for the men to put their pole into (I did warn you), usually filling the hole with stones so that the pole will stand up straight. Many multicolored ribbons are hung from the top of the pole, and the folks all gather around and dance in opposite directions, intertwining the ribbons as they go to symbolize, well, you know …

Naturally, the dance never goes quite as planned, and the weaving often ends up lopsided, but that's half the fun.

In a permanent Pagan community, a May queen and king are often chosen by lot (a small pebble in a cupcake is pretty common) and will serve for the year until Beltane rolls around again.

If you are a Solitary Witch and there is no local group with which you can celebrate, then just crown yourself queen (or king) for the day. After all, who's to stop you?

If you can join together with a group or the area Pagan community, then make the most of this wonderful day—put on your sexiest garb, grab a partner and a bottle of mead, and dance to your heart's content. Because *heart* is what this holiday is all about.

Witch Wit:

"*Burn, Baby, Burn*"

How do you make a Witch's martini?
Replace the olive with a toasted nut!

Ask Onyx:
"Beltane Blues"

Dear Onyx,

   I usually love Beltane, but this year I am single, and I am a little bummed about hanging around all those couples at our local Beltane gathering. Should I just stay home?

   Lonely in Los Angeles

Dear Lonely,

   Don't you dare! Beltane isn't just for lovers—it celebrates love in all its forms. So go to that gathering, dress up in your coolest garb, and enjoy being with your friends. Have fun, dance around the Maypole with whoever is handy, and don't forget to flirt! Remember—if you can't be with the one you love, then love the one you're with!

   Bright blessings,
   Onyx

If you have ever said, "Oh, I wish I didn't have _____" (fill in the blank with whatever is appropriate: these extra ten pounds, this dreary depression, ten thousand dollars in debt), then what you need is a banishing spell. No, a banishing spell will not magickally get rid of the extra weight or the credit card debt you ran up—at least, not all by itself. What it *will* do is help you to start working on those things in a concrete fashion and set you on your path toward improving your life.

Banishing spells are best done during the dark or new moon, since that is a good time for decrease, rather than increase. And keep in mind that you can only use banishing magick to affect yourself—no trying to banish the noisy neighbors in 2B (although you could trying banishing the annoyance you feel).

Banishing can be used for any issue where you feel you need help letting go of something. For instance, if you are having problems with your health, you can do an illness-banishing spell at the new moon, followed by a spell to increase health at the full moon. Two sides of the same coin, if you will. Here is an example of a spell I wrote for just that purpose:

> *Banish strife and banish pain*
> *Bring balance to the world again*
> *Pain and illness soon depart*
> *Peace comes to the willing heart*
> *With ease let go of ills and woes*
> *Let health increase as this moon grows.*

Remember that as with all other magick, you need to follow up with concrete actions in the real world. It is not enough to say "I am going to banish illness"—you then need to go out there and do whatever you can to back up the energy you put out into the universe through your magickal work. But sometimes when everyday actions on their own aren't enough, a banishing spell can give you that extra magickal oomph to make your wishes come true.

Magic the Cat's Simple Spells:
"Banishing Act"

For a simple banishing spell, write whatever you want to banish on a slip of paper, then light a small bonfire (outside) or use a fireproof dish (inside). Focus all your intent on ridding yourself of the to-be-banished thing, and say the following as you place the paper in the fire: "Banish this as I desire! Banish now into the fire!" Then burn it to bits, baby.

Magic's Herbal Helpers:
"Basil Basics"

Basil is another one of those herbs that is more widely known for its use in the kitchen than it is for its magickal properties. (Hey, what they don't know won't hurt them.) But as Witches, we know that basil is also referred to as Witches' herb and used for purification, protection, and love magick. It is also great for use in prosperity rituals. So the next time you make up a batch of pesto, mutter a spell under your breath while you do it—and before you can say "Kitchen Witch," you'll be doing basic basil magick. Bon appetit!

BURNING TIMES

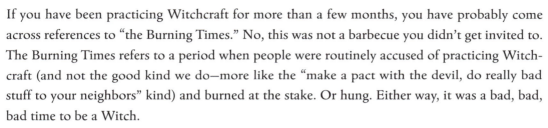

If you have been practicing Witchcraft for more than a few months, you have probably come across references to "the Burning Times." No, this was not a barbecue you didn't get invited to. The Burning Times refers to a period when people were routinely accused of practicing Witchcraft (and not the good kind we do—more like the "make a pact with the devil, do really bad stuff to your neighbors" kind) and burned at the stake. Or hung. Either way, it was a bad, bad, bad time to be a Witch.

Unfortunately, it was a bad, bad, bad time to be a bunch of other people, too. Not all of those who were accused and executed were Witches; in fact, many scholars believe that only a small percentage of the victims were truly followers of the Craft or any other type of Pagan worship. Among those who died were also midwives, healers, single women who lived alone (especially if they owned property), people against whom neighbors had a grudge, innocents who were accused by other victims after torture, and other folks who just happened to be in the wrong place at the wrong time. The worst of the Burning Times happened between 1550 and 1650, although the executions didn't end completely until 1792 in Europe and 1830 in America. There are various theories on the number of people who died: anywhere from 50,000 on up to 9 million. Modern historical studies suggest that a relatively accurate estimate of the number of people who were killed ends up at around 40,000. Either way, it was a sad time of mass murder, paranoia, and righteousness (or should that be *wrong*eousness?).

Much of the killing was instigated by the Catholic Church but carried out by smaller local courts. During this time, most of the remaining Witches (who would probably have referred to themselves as healers or "charmers," since "Witch" as a positive term is a relatively new invention) were driven underground or gave up practicing altogether in order to stay alive. The end result was the same: valuable knowledge was lost forever, and Witchcraft went underground. Until now. These days, we are (more or less) free to practice in the open, but residual beliefs and prejudices from this time still exist. It is important that we never forget what was lost, nor take for granted our freedom to practice what we believe. May the Burning Times never come again.

Great Gods!
"Brigit's Bounty"

Brigit is a Celtic goddess of smithcraft, fire, poetry, and healing. Also known as Brighid, Brigid, and Bride, her name is actually pronounced "Breed" or "Bree" (there is nothing like a Celtic name to confuse the heck out of you). Brigit's day was commonly celebrated on Imbolc (February 2), and she is still the goddess we invoke most often at rituals held on that day.

She was so beloved in her native Ireland that the Christians turned her into St. Brigit of Kildare rather than try to outlaw her worship altogether. Nice try, guys—she's still one of ours!

Food of the Gods:
"Bread Basket"

Bread is the perfect food to take to any Pagan feast. Not only is it made from grains, which symbolize the earth, but breaking bread together is an age-old way to celebrate friendship and community.

There is a wonderful bread recipe in *The Wicca Cookbook: Recipes, Ritual, and Lore* by Jamie Wood and Tara Seefeldt called Brigid's Magical Bread. (According to the authors, it is the perfect bread to bake if you are trying to win someone's love.) Or you could bake challah, the Jewish bread that braids three pieces of dough together—a perfect symbol for the triple goddess.

coven

Craft

Crone

colors

cakes and ale

correspondences

candles

Charge of the Goddess

C

COVEN

There are basically two different kinds of Witches: Solitaries, who practice alone, and group Witches, who practice, well, with a group. (Okay, there are actually lots of different kinds of Witches, but this is a small book, so just work with me here.)

Those Witches who practice together may call their group by any of a number of different names, but the most common and traditional type is known as a coven.

Merriam-Webster's Collegiate Dictionary defines a coven (from the Latin for "to agree") as "a collection of individuals with similar interests or activities"—and if that isn't a description of a group of Witches (especially the "collection of individuals" part), then I don't know what is.

Historically, a coven usually consisted of thirteen members, but these days it can be any number from three on up to however many can fit into your living room and still get along for more than twenty minutes. (So, three.)

Covens were traditionally led by a high priest and a high priestess, and often contained members who were at different levels in a degree system, some more advanced than others. These days, covens are less likely to have such rigid hierarchies (although there are some folks who are more comfortable with the traditional forms, and there is not a darned thing wrong with that) and often have only a high priestess or a high priest and not both.

The truth is, it is not all that easy to find a group of fellow fliers to practice with, so modern-day Witches often create the best group they can with whoever and whatever works.

The important thing to remember about a coven is that it is not enough to just get together and dance naked under the moon (although that's not a bad place to start, come to think of it). A coven is a serious spiritual commitment and one not meant to be made lightly. Many groups will practice together for a year and a day before making that final formal commitment to each other.

On the other hand, once you have found (or created from scratch) a coven of your own, there is nothing more rewarding than joining with your witchy family and dancing, singing, and celebrating under the moon—together in heart, mind, and soul.

Required Reading:
"Circle, Coven & Grove: A Year of Magickal Practice"

If you are going to be starting a coven, or if the coven you are in doesn't have anyone who is comfortable writing rituals, check out my first book, *Circle, Coven & Grove*. Oh, hell—check it out anyway! *Circle, Coven & Grove* contains a year of rituals for new moons, full moons, and sabbats, as well as suggestions for practicing as a group, ritual etiquette, correspondences, and more. And, yes, it works for Solitary Witches, too.

CRAFT

You probably already know that Wicca is often referred to as the Craft, but have you ever thought about what that means?

Obviously it is short for Witchcraft, a more general term for all the various types of witchy practices, but why call it Witchcraft, as opposed to Witchhood, or Witchness, or something else along those lines?

The word *craft* is both a noun and a verb (that is to say, both a thing and an action). If we return to our Merriam-Webster's dictionary, we will see that *craft* is defined as the following: "skill in planning, making, and executing," "an occupation or trade requiring manual dexterity or artistic skill," "the members of a trade or trade association," or (and here's my favorite) "to make or produce with care, skill, or ingenuity."

All of these describe some element of being a Witch, but I think that it is the last definition that is the most important. Being a Witch is not just about who you are ("I am a Witch") but also about what you do and how you do it.

Our rituals are carefully crafted to evoke both reverence and mirth *and* to achieve our goals. Many of us craft some of our tools (the tools of our trade, if you will) or various components of our magickal work: oils, charms, candles, runestone sets, and more. I have known talented and crafty Witches who have made their own chalices from clay or embroidered the Wiccan Rede to hang above their altars.

The important thing to remember is that whatever you do as a Witch should be done with care and with your whole heart. Not everyone is Martha Stewart (who I'm pretty sure is not a Witch), but even the artistically challenged can set up a simple but beautiful altar and say a heartfelt prayer out beneath the light of the full moon.

That, after all, really is why it is called Witchcraft.

CRONE

In the mundane world, when people use the word *crone,* they usually envision a shriveled old woman, bent and wrinkled. It is not a compliment. If you're a woman and you overhear your blind date referring to you on his cell phone as an old crone, feel free to hit him with your purse. Hard.

But in the Pagan world, the word *crone* has a completely different meaning. Well, three meanings, actually.

The first meaning is the one that most of us might think of automatically—the crone as the representation of the third embodiment of the triple goddess: maiden, mother, and crone. When the goddess is in her crone guise (such as at Samhain), she has reached the end of the year and the end of a cycle. Wrinkled she may be, but also wise and revered. And as Pagans, we know that eventually this phase too will pass, and the goddess will come around again as maiden, young and beautiful.

The word *crone* is also used to indicate age and honor in the practice of Witchcraft. A crone is a woman (sorry, guys, but there is no male equivalent—I guess you'll just have to settle for being called "that old, wise Pagan dude") who has practiced the Craft for many years and has attained much wisdom and experience along the way. To be called a crone in this context really is a compliment, a term of respect and honor. Personally, I look forward to the day when I am called a crone!

Crone can also be an indication of the stage of a woman's life. Once a witchy woman has hit menopause (or it has hit her), she is no longer considered to be in the mother stage of her life and has moved on to the status of crone.

Despite what you might think, this is not a bad thing.

Remember that it is only in our modern world that "old" has become a bad word. In days gone by, the older generation was more often looked up to and admired for their knowledge and their wisdom. The Pagan community as a whole is much more likely to still do so.

So if you are a woman of a certain age, enjoy being a crone. Rather than bemoan what you have lost (remember, it will all come along again in your next life), rejoice at what you have gained—wisdom and knowledge and the ability to lord them over the younger generation. Be proud to be a crone; you've earned it!

Witch 101:
"How to Know if You're a Crone"

1. You can't remember the original color of your hair, so you just keep dying it to match your garb.

2. All the young Witches treat you with respect—even if your own kids don't.

3. Your hot flashes are so bad, your coven skips the bonfire and just stands next to you.

4. You hold the midnight ritual at eight so that you can go to bed early.

5. When people talk about worshipping the Old Ones, everyone turns to look at you.

Witches use color all the time when doing magick. Each color is associated with specific magickal qualities and essential tasks.

For instance, yellow is the color used for the element of air ~~(west)~~ East. And since air is the element associated with the intellect, yellow is the color for magickal work pertaining to the mind, such as intelligence, wisdom, creativity, communication, and anything to do with mental abilities. So if you wanted to do a spell to help you do well on a test, you would burn a yellow candle or wear a yellow shirt (or whatever). In addition, because of its brightness, yellow is used for joy and the sun.

Red is the color used for the element of fire (south). It is used in any magickal work pertaining to fire, but also for passion, lust, courage, sexual love (and sometimes for the romantic kind, not that they are necessarily mutually exclusive), energy, strength, and willpower.

Blue is the color used for the element of water (west). Use it for healing, peace, truth, justice, sleep, dreams, serenity, hope, and psychic abilities. Some Witches use different shades of blue for different tasks, such as light blue for peace, bright blue for protection, dark blue for justice, and indigo for meditation—personally, I think that you might as well use whichever blue seems most suitable to you at the time (or that you happen to have on hand).

Green is the color used for the element of earth (north), although some people use brown for this as well. Green is used in magick done for prosperity, growth, abundance, luck, fertility, success, and gardens. Brown is good for stability, animals, strength, grounding, and any kind of earth magick.

Among other colors, Witches also use black (divination, banishing, protection, binding and absorbing negative energy, and any kind of crone magick), purple (psychic ability, insight, dreams, spirituality, inner strength, wisdom, divination, and magickal work), silver (the goddess, the moon, spirit, or anything feminine), gold (the god, the sun, power, and anything masculine), pink (love, friendship, romance, harmony, spring), and white (clarity, purification, truth, hope).

A white candle can always be used if you don't have the color that you want; you simply visualize the appropriate color in your mind instead.

These are the most common uses for each of the better-known colors, but every book you read will differ at least slightly, and some Witchcraft traditions can vary quite widely in how they use colors. My suggestion for this, as with all else that you do with the Craft, is to follow your heart and listen to your intuition. If you are doing a spell for prosperity, and you feel that it would be best to use a yellow candle instead of a green one, who am I to say you're wrong? It's your magick; you can color it any way you want to!

Helpful Hints:
"Color Under Where?!"

There are many ways to integrate color magick into your life, but here is one of the simplest and most fun. One of the women in my circle picks the color of her underwear for the day based on whatever magickal boost she feels she's going to need the most. Blue for healing, green for prosperity, pink for love or compassion, black for protection, red for energy...or passion! You get the picture. It's a little bit of magick you can do every day, and no one needs to know but you. And, hey, it's an excuse to buy more cool underwear! (You can even buy some for your honey...!)

Seems pretty self-explanatory, doesn't it? You've got your cakes; you've got your ale. End of story. Or is it?

What is "cakes and ale," and why is it a part of any major magickal ritual? And does it actually *have* to be a cake and ale? What if you're on a diet or don't like the taste of beer?

Cakes and ale is the generic term we use to describe the ceremony at the end of the ritual where we have a bite or two to eat and a little something to drink. We do this partially to replenish the energy we used in doing magick, but it mostly serves to ground us and bring us back from the altered state we entered during ritual.

Food and drink serve as a link to the "real world" and a representation of the bounty given to us by the gods. Some Witches consider cakes and ale to be a sacrament of sorts, through which we take in a token of the divine energy of the goddess and god. If you are practicing with a group, the high priestess and/or high priest will bless and consecrate the cakes and ale before they are passed from hand to hand around the circle.

Quintessential Quotes:
"Cakes and Ale Communion"

Eating kicks your body into a different mode. Since food is a product of the earth, it gently returns our awareness to the physical reality. Food is a manifestation of divine energy. Eating is a form of communion.
—Scott Cunningham, *Wicca: A Guide for the Solitary Practitioner*

The symbol of breaking bread together has served to connect people throughout history, and the sharing of cakes and ale can be remarkably moving. Many of the groups that I have practiced with say, as they pass the cakes, "May you never hunger" or "May you always have plenty to eat and someone to share it with."

And no, it doesn't have to be cake. I have used everything from actual cake or cookies to apples, strawberries, or sesame-seed crackers. And the ale is often wine but can easily be fruit juice or even water instead. Witches often try to choose something for cakes and ale that is appropriate to the season, such as seed cake in the spring or cider in the fall.

The only truly important component of cakes and ale is your mindful appreciation of the earth's gifts and your reverence for the ritual itself. In short—eat, drink, and be merry!

Correspondences

Look in almost any basic book about Witchcraft and you will find a list of correspondences. Some books are little more than a compilation of such lists. But very few books tell you why we use them—and when it is better to do without.

Correspondences are a handy tool, no question about it. The idea has existed since the dawn of time (and no, I wasn't there personally!) that there are associations between various objects, symbols, names, and forces, and that one thing can stand for another. One of the most important tenets of Witchcraft—"As above, so below"—reminds us that what we do on the physical plane can affect the ethereal plane (and vice versa).

You can look at correspondences as a list of ingredients for use in preparing a magickal dish. For any given spell, there is a matching set of possible correspondences. Here's an example: if you are doing a ritual to bring in prosperity, the best day of the week is Thursday, the candle color is green, the herb is basil, and so on.

So here's the question: what if you need to do a prosperity spell right away, and it is a Friday, you only have white candles, and you ate the last of your basil on a salad for lunch? Does this mean that you can't do the spell?

Don't be silly. (Well, okay, be silly if you want, it's not like I can actually stop you.) Correspondences are a tool that we use to help us focus our will and put our intentions into a more concrete form, but they're completely optional. Sometimes the strongest magick is nothing more than a heartfelt plea to the gods for help, or a single candle and a quiet chant in a darkened room.

By all means, go ahead and use correspondences when you do a ritual. But don't forget that what really matters is what's in your heart—and the gods can see that even on a Tuesday with no candles at all.

Candles

Candles have been used throughout human history in the context of spiritual and magickal work. They symbolize light in the midst of darkness, serve as an offering to deity, and can be used in conjunction with other symbols to focus energy and intent.

Witches often choose a candle whose color corresponds to the spell being done (something I talk about in the sections on color and correspondences, which you have memorized, of course), inscribe the candle with runes or other symbols and/or anoint the candles with magickally charged oils.

Candles are used to mark the four quarters of the circle during ritual, and are lit in honor of the god and goddess. They can also be used as a focal point for meditation. And, of course, they shed light, which can come in very handy when you are doing a ritual outside or in a darkened room. (Note to those who practice skyclad: hot wax on bare skin can be very distracting, not to mention painful. You may want to be extra careful when working around candles naked. Note to Witches who like to wear garb with long, flowing sleeves: you need to be even more careful than the naked Witches. We've finally gotten everybody else to stop burning Witches—no point in setting ourselves on fire!)

Any kinds of candles may be used for magickal work, although some people believe that candles made of natural materials such as beeswax are best. You can buy candles in the shape of animals or people, candles with gemstones embedded in them, or candles that are already consecrated and blessed for magickal use.

I have made my own candles, adding oils and other natural materials and concentrating on my magickal goals from start to finish. For those Witches with the time and inclination to do such a thing, I recommend it highly. But there is nothing wrong with using the simplest white candle from the dollar store as long as you use it with perfect love and perfect trust.

CHARGE OF THE GODDESS

No, this is not the bill from when the goddess went shopping at Nordstrom's. Nor is it what the goddess says when leading her troops into battle, although I can picture that...

The Charge of the Goddess is probably the single best-known work of Pagan writing and the most beautiful. It comes in many versions, some poetry and some prose, and there is much debate on who wrote it and when. (And you know that when I say "much debate" about something Pagan, that's really saying something.)

Some people say that Gerald Gardner wrote it back in the 1950s, either with Doreen Valiente or by himself. Gardner apparently said that he based his version on ancient sources that had been handed down throughout the centuries, but there is some (well, okay, a lot of) doubt about the validity of that claim. Others say Valiente wrote it by herself.

It has been adapted and rewritten by such notable Witches as Janet and Stewart Farrar and Starhawk, and one version or another can be found in many books on Witchcraft as well as online.

Personally, I don't care who wrote it. I only care that it moves me to tears almost every time I read it—it is that beautiful.

The Charge of the Goddess represents a speech by the goddess to her witchy followers and is often read as a part of the drawing down the moon ritual. It is usually spoken by the high priestess or high priest, but it certainly doesn't have to be—if you are Solitary, try standing outside under the full moon sometime and reading it out loud. I think that you will see what I mean.

So find a version that speaks to your heart, and as the Charge says, "Listen to the words of the Great Mother, who of old was called Artemis, Astarte, Dione, Melusine, Aphrodite, Ceridwen, Diana, Arionrhod, Brigid, and by many other names..."

Stoned!
"Carnelian Caresses"

Carnelian is one of my favorite stones. It varies in color from a sunny orange to a deep brick red, but all its shades are lovely. It is a form of chalcedony and was worn in ancient Egypt to quiet anger, envy, and hate. Modern Witches use it to create peace and harmony, ease depression, boost courage and self-confidence, and counter negative thoughts. Who doesn't have the occasional day when *that* wouldn't come in handy?

Carnelian is also said to confer patience and help in cleansing the physical body. It is used in relationship work, both because it is helpful in removing the traits that keep us separate and lonely and because it is one of the best gem-stones for sex magick. (Maybe it's the self-confidence thing.) It is also ground-ing, which could be handy after the sex magick…

Ask Magic the Cat:
"Cat Magick"

Dear Magic the Cat,

As a familiar, I know that you are probably an expert at cat magick, but I am new at this stuff, and my Witch doesn't have a clue. Can you give me a few "cat magick basics" to pass on to her?

Flustered Feline in Florida

Dear Flustered,

Don't worry your little whiskers about it—cat magick is easy! Just tell your Witch to invoke the Egyptian goddess Bastet; use some catnip and a piece of tiger's-eye. You'll soon be the most magickal cat in the 'hood. And if you're lucky, maybe some of the catnip will fall on the floor...

Familiarly,
Magic the Cat

Magickal Must-Haves:
"Chants"

In *The Encyclopedia of Witches & Witchcraft,* Rosemary Ellen Guiley defines *chanting* as "the repetition of sacred or magical words, names, and phrases as a way of altering consciousness and raising psychic power."[5]

This is one of the simplest yet most effective and beautiful chants in the witchy world:

> *The earth,*
> *The air,*
> *The fire,*
> *The water,*
> *Return, return, return.*

Chants are tough to learn if you don't hear them in person, but there are more and more sites online that have examples of beautiful witchy chants, complete with words and music. Or go to a Pagan festival sometime, and learn them from your fellow fliers!

---

5   Page 51.

In the Witch's Tool Chest:
"Cauldron and Chalice—My Cup Runneth Over"

Many of the tools that Witches use are said to represent either the masculine (the god) or the feminine (the goddess). Two of the most common "female" tools are the cauldron and the chalice. Because of their cupped shape, they symbolize the womb of the goddess.

Who isn't familiar with the image of the Witch stirring up some magickal potion in her cauldron? (Okay, I think most of the time it was probably just her dinner, but who are we to argue with centuries of fairy tales?) These days, Witches are more likely to use the cauldron—usually an iron pot with three legs—to hold a fire during ritual or just for decoration. The Celtic goddess Ceridwen was famous for her cauldron, in which she brewed the mead of wisdom and inspiration. (Don't you wish you had that recipe?)

The chalice is used to hold the wine or water for use during ritual, and it represents the feminine forces of intuition, understanding, and receptivity. They are often made of silver, glass, pewter, or pottery. I think it is important to choose a chalice that you truly love the look and feel of, and set it aside for use during rituals only. Somehow using that Batman juice glass doesn't seem to cut it.

Magic's Herbal Helpers:
"Calendula and Chamomile Comforts"

Calendula and chamomile are two of my Witch's favorite magickal herbs. Although they are used for different magickal tasks, they are both considered to be comforters, soothing in nature.

Calendula (also known as Bride of the Sun and pot marigold) is used for love and clairvoyance magick (or maybe clairvoyance about love? Man, would THAT be handy!). The common marigold that you see in gardens is easy to grow, and you can save the seeds for midwinter magick and then plant them in the spring to see your dreams grow. Calendula is also a wonderful medicinal herb and can be made into a soothing salve for world-weary skin.

Chamomile (also called ground apple) is used for prosperity, peace, and sleep magick. You can add it to meditation incenses or put it in a charm to draw money. A cup of chamomile tea will also help you sleep, so that you can dream of all the things you'll do with your newfound wealth...

Great Gods!
"Cernunnos"

Cernunnos is a Celtic god whose name means "horned one." God of the hunt and fertility, he is often pictured as a man with the antlers of a stag and referred to as the Horned God.

Cernunnos is the Celtic god of the Underworld as well, and rules over the gates between life and death. As such, he is a fitting god to invoke at Samhain, when the veil between the worlds is at its thinnest. Not only a Celtic god, Cernunnos was also worshipped by the Romans and the Gauls. (The gall of them!)

The Horned God is the deity of animals and is known for his ability to transform himself into any animal shape instantaneously. So if you're out in the woods and meet a deer, be polite ... because you just never know.

Food of the Gods:
"Chocolate Lovers, Unite!"

Here's an interesting thought: chocolate is an herb. No, seriously. The Hershey bar you had for breakfast (what, you thought nobody knew?) came from a tree called *Theobroma cacao*. The word *Theobroma* means "food of the gods," which seems pretty appropriate to me.

Chocolate in one form or another has been used in magickal work since the time of the Aztecs, and maybe before. (Any bets on what Eve *really* used to tempt Adam?) It is primarily used for love magick and is said to increase our ability to give and receive love. As long as it also increases our ability to give and receive more chocolate...

If you want a really fun ritual to do, look online for the "Chocolate Ritual." All chocolate, the whole thing, from start to finish. What do you mean, am I kidding? I would never joke about chocolate!

drumming

dedication

divination

drawing down
the moon

days of the week

Demeter

D

DRUMMING

You might not think to add it to your list of required Pagan tools, but a drum is as vital to many Witches as an athame or a chalice.

Pagans in every culture you can name have used some sort of music to help them focus, celebrate, and commune with the gods. Flutes, rattles, and simple stringed instruments are common, but almost every Pagan-based society—from Native Americans to ancient Celts to the smallest African village—has used drumming as a part of their spiritual practice.

There is something about the rhythm and resonance of a drum that touches the human heart, maybe because it too sounds a bit like a drum (ta-dum, ta-dum, ta-dum). Drumming can induce a trance state, focus meditation, and build up energy within a witchy circle. There is nothing like drumming to express joy during a celebration, since you can dance to it, sing to it, and just plain have fun with it.

Anyone can drum. You don't have to have musical talent or even a sense of rhythm (although it helps). Besides, when the whole group is drumming, no one can tell if you are just a little bit out of sync...

Quintessential Quotes:
"Dancing in the Dark"

Dance is certainly an ancient ritual practice. It is also a magical act, for physical movement releases energy from the body—the same energy used in magic.

—Scott Cunningham, Wicca

And drums are cheap and easy to make. While some folks have beautiful, expensive, wildly ornate drums (and there is nothing wrong with that), you can just as easily make do with a simple pottery drum or Celtic bodhran (a flat Irish drum made from goatskin and beaten with a stick instead of the hand). Or make your own from an empty container. Anything you can beat on that will make a hollow sound can be used as a drum.

So the next time the drumming starts, make sure that you are ready to join in. Beat your drum and lose yourself in ageless rhythms and spiritual bliss, submerging your soul in the Pagan music of the heart.

Dedication

Some might say that it takes dedication to be a Witch. And they would be right in more ways than one.

When a Witch says that he or she is dedicated to the Craft, it might just mean that she or he puts in a lot of time and effort. More likely, though, they are referring to a particular ceremony called a dedication.

A dedication is a formal declaration of intent, a wedding vow of sorts, if you will, that binds the Witch to the practice of Witchcraft or to a coven or group. While not necessarily a vow of the "'til death do us part" sort (since you can always change your mind and take up Buddhism instead, if you like), it is a serious commitment and should never be made lightly.

Some Witches know right away that they want to make this commitment, and some practice for their entire lives without ever making a formal dedication—neither way is right or wrong. In truth, the only "wrong" way is to make a dedication frivolously, without thinking it through first.

Otherwise, there are a number of ways to go about it. If you are a Solitary Witch, there are lots of great self-dedication rituals available in books or online. Better yet, just light some candles, cast your circle, and speak from the heart—the gods will certainly hear you.

If you are in a group, your high priest and/or high priestess will probably dedicate you, usually with the rest of the group there to help out and bear witness. You can even invite friends and family as long as they will treat the event with the proper reverence.

A group dedication is a slightly different event—if your group is just starting out, you will probably hold a ritual that dedicates you all at the same time.

No matter what kind of dedication you are doing, the ritual will be beautiful, moving, and will change your life forever. Who could ask for more?

Elemental Essentials:
"Dedicated to You"

Here is a simple dedication ritual. On the night of a full moon, go outside and draw a circle around yourself with your athame. Once you are inside your circle, light a white candle and gaze at it until you can feel the moonlight filling your soul. Then pour a libation to the goddess from your chalice onto the ground. Hold the chalice up to the moon and say, "With all my heart and soul, I, _____, willingly dedicate myself to the Craft and to you. So mote it be." Drink from the chalice, and then sit quietly in your circle until it feels like the right time to go back inside.

Divination may be defined as the art and craft of seeking hidden knowledge or foretelling future events through intuition, the interpretation of omens and signs, or with the aid of outside powers.

I ask you: how cool is that!

Most Witches I know practice one form of divination or another. Some use a number of different methods, which can include such tools as tarot cards, runes, astrology, and the I Ching. There are probably even some folks out there who still use chicken bones. (How do you use chicken bones to do divination? Well, first you catch your chicken...)

With the aforementioned methods, the various tools (cards, stones, etc.) are used to channel or boost the user's own intuitive abilities. Some techniques, like looking into a crystal ball or a scrying mirror, take this even further by using a blank surface as a tool to project images that are truly seen only by the mind's eye. (The scrying mirror has the added advantage of being black, so it doesn't reflect that damned pimple on your forehead.)

Even dreams can be used for divination. Some Witches always keep a dream diary by the bed and some dream-boosting herbs under their pillows.

The best way to get started, if you have never tried divination before, is to pick whichever method appeals to you most and just start trying. A few lessons from a more experienced fellow Witch are always helpful, but all you really need are a pack of cards or a bag of runes and an open mind.

Some people are naturally more intuitive (or downright psychic) than others, but I believe that almost anyone can do basic divination if they try.

And as a bonus, most card decks are gorgeous and interesting in their own right, and runes made of inexpensive gemstones are stunningly beautiful when spilling out of a simple velvet bag. So run out and pick up a few fun tools and the books to go with them. I predict that you'll have a great time!

Magic the Cat's Simple Spells:
"Divine Divination"

Here is a great spell from my Witch's book *Circle, Coven & Grove* called "Spell to Open the Inner Eye." It is meant to help you with divination, no matter which tool you choose to use.

On the night of a full moon, light a white candle, focus all your attention on your wish to open yourself to intuition, and say the following:

> *Moon, moon, burning bright*
> *Help me hone my inner sight*
> *Make my vision clear and true*
> *Show me what I need to do*
> *Whether cards or stones of old*
> *Show me what I need to know*
> *Guide my heart and guide my hand*
> *Help me see and understand.*

Drawing Down the Moon

Okay, nobody actually expects you to draw down the moon. For one thing, think of the tidal waves! *Drawing down the moon* is a term that Witches use for an act of ritual magick during which a high priestess channels the essence of the goddess, inviting her into the circle.

This is a ritual that has been around for a long time; there are references to drawing or calling down the moon in ancient Greek and Roman writing, and the rite itself can be seen on pottery from that era. But as old as it is, the ritual is as meaningful today as it ever was.

One of the basic tenets of Witchcraft that makes it different from the religions that most of us were raised in is that each of us has a personal connection to the divine. We all contain the spark of deity within us. So it is not such a stretch to think that any one of us could, if so moved, provide a temporary vessel for the gods to speak through.

This is what happens during the ritual of drawing down the moon. The high priestess, sometimes after fasting and meditation, opens herself spiritually so that the goddess may enter her and speak, well, whatever it is the goddess has to say at the time. Traditionally, the high priest of a coven called upon the goddess as the high priestess stood ready. These days, if there is no high priest, the high priestess will invoke the goddess herself, often through the use of a magickal poem called the Charge of the Goddess.

There is also a male counterpart called drawing down the sun, or drawing down the Horned God, but it is not used nearly as often. And, of course, if you are a Solitary Witch, you can simply draw down the moon by yourself.

Either way, should you decide to invite the goddess in, remember to do so with reverence and appreciation. And don't be surprised if you are never quite the same again...

Days of the Week

You know them, you love them: Monday, Tuesday, Wednesday...okay, maybe you don't love Monday so much. Perhaps you are a bit fonder of Friday. But what if you want to do magick for business success—which day do you like the best then?

As it turns out, probably either Sunday or Thursday.

Each day of the week corresponds to a different planetary energy and a different type of magick, so you may want to choose carefully when picking a day on which to perform your next ritual. Of course, if you read ten books, they may each give you slightly different correspondences for each day—welcome to the wonderful world of Witchcraft!

So how do you decide when to do your ritual? Look at the lists, check out your books, then do what feels right, the same as always. But just to get you started, here is a basic list for each day:

Sunday—The sun, business/professional success, power, friendship, change, healing, joy.

Monday—The moon, home, family, faery magick, gardening, psychic work, female issues (because of the moon's influence, this is a good time to do goddess work, too).

Tuesday—Mars, victory, strength, athletics, passion, sex, masculine issues (see a trend here? Mars was the god of war...also, he got around).

Wednesday—Mercury, communication, creativity, wisdom, writing, study, self-improvement (remember that Mercury was the winged messenger of the gods and this starts to make sense).

Thursday—Jupiter, prosperity, good luck, success, legal issues, joy.

Friday—Venus, comfort, love, friendship, romance, beauty (you can see where Venus comes in here, can't you?).

Saturday—Saturn, mysteries, wisdom, reincarnation, exorcism, banishing disease, endings.

Of course, if it is a Friday and you *really* need to do prosperity work, you can still go ahead and do it. As with all correspondences, these are only one component of magickal work, and how you choose to use them—or whether you use them at all—is up to you. You're the Witch, after all. Even on Mondays...

DEMETER

Ancient Pagans lived on the land and used their spiritual beliefs as a way to explain the changes in the world around them. Probably the best-known example of this is the Greek story of Demeter and her daughter Persephone (known respectively as Ceres and Kore to the Romans).

Demeter is a mother goddess and the goddess of grain. In the Greek pantheon, she was responsible for keeping the earth green and abundant. She did her job very well, too, until she had a Very Bad Day.

On that day, Hades, the god of the Underworld, saw Persephone picking flowers in a field and kidnapped her, bringing her down to the land of the dead to be his queen. (What, he never heard of a first date? Maybe a little chocolate?)

Demeter roamed the world searching for her daughter, neglecting her duties and bringing really bad weather to the earth. People were upset. (Starving will do that to you.) So Zeus ordered Hades to return Persephone to her mother, so the woman could get her mind back on her job. Unfortunately, Persephone had eaten a few pomegranate seeds during her stay Down Under, so she was forced to return for a few months every year. During this time, Demeter mourns and the earth is no longer fruitful.

Here in upstate New York, we call that winter.

Witch 101:
"Deosil or Widdershins?"

I love the use of archaic (that is, really darned old and not in common use anymore) terms in the practice of Witchcraft—I think it gives us a feeling of connection to the Witches who have gone before us. But it can get confusing, too. Two of the most apt-to-befuddle terms are *deosil* and *widdershins* (also sometimes seen as windershins). These are both used to tell us which direction to turn in when we are moving in circle. Deosil (DEE-oh-sill or JESS-il) means to turn clockwise, or sunwise. Widdershins (WID-der-shins) is the opposite, or counterclockwise.

Almost all movement inside a magickal circle is done deosil. We cast the circle moving to the right, and once in circle we continue to move in that direction—so that if you get up to go to the altar, for instance, you then continue moving all the way around the circle until you come back to your place. Widdershins is only used to undo things, so it may be used at the end of a ritual to open the circle space or in doing any magick for "undoing" (such as unbinding spells).

esbats

elements

ESBATS

Esbats are at the very core of the practice of Witchcraft. Esbats are the full moons, of which there are thirteen a year. Even if you do nothing else as a Witch, you should probably do something special on full moon nights.

Esbat celebrations can be as simple as walking outside, standing under the light of the moon, and basking in the glow of the goddess. (If it's raining, just use your imagination—the moon's still up there somewhere...)

Alternately, many Witches use this night for full-on ritual: casting the circle, calling the quarters, lighting the candles, and doing serious spellwork. Most Pagan groups meet on this night every month, and many Witches harness the extra power of the full moon to boost their most serious magickal workings.

Whichever approach you choose to take, remember that the full moon is the symbol of the goddess in all her bright glory. So whether you party or get serious about your spellcraft (or both), don't forget to say a reverent greeting and heartfelt thank-you to the lady we all worship.

Then light the candles, fire up the bonfire, and dance under the stars with your cat, your friends, or the faeries in your garden. Just be sure if you're going skyclad (that is to say, naked) that there is nobody watching whom you'd rather *not* have seeing either your ritual or your cellulite...

Ask Onyx:
"Esbat, Sabbat, What's What?"

Dear Onyx,

I've been practicing Witchcraft for a few years now, but I still get confused between esbats and sabbats. Is there an easy way to keep them straight?

Befuddled in Buffalo

Dear Befuddled,

These words drive many Witches batty, at least in the beginning. Try using a mnemonic trick to keep them straight, like *esbats* (full moons) are *essential* to the goddess, while *sabbats* (holidays) are for *celebration*. Hope that helps!

Bright blessings,
Onyx

ELEMENTS

What do earth, air, fire, and water have in common? It's elementary, my dear Watson.

All four are called elements and their use is everywhere in witchy practices.

Each element corresponds to a quarter when used in Pagan rituals (the quarters are the four directions—north, south, east, and west—each of which corresponds to an element), and each also has various colors and properties that are associated with it. For instance:

Earth—The north quarter. Usually associated with the color green (although some use brown), it is said to be grounding and is associated with the physical body, the home, and practical matters. You can use anything earthy to represent this element on your altar, even a small plant, but I like to use a rock or gemstone crystal.

Air—The east quarter. Associated with the color yellow (so if you are using candles at each of the four quarters in your circle, this is the color for that quarter—see how this works?) and the intellect and communication. It is usually represented on the altar by a feather or incense, since the smoke from the incense floats up through the air to the gods.

Fire—The south quarter. Associated with the color red, creativity, and passion (whoo, baby!), fire can be represented on the altar by a burning candle or a small cauldron.

Water—The west quarter (if you have trouble remembering which one is which, as most of us do in the beginning, try remembering water=west, air=east, since the sounds are close). Associated with the color blue, the emotions, and intuition (things that are always fluid and ever-changing). Water is usually represented on the altar by, well, water. (Duh.) You can put some out in a bowl or a special container, or use a shell instead if you want.

These four elements show up in almost every aspect of day-to-day Witchcraft, but it is important to remember that there is a fifth element that we recognize as well, and that is the element of spirit. This element is what binds the other four together, as indeed it binds us all to each other. And of all the elements that you use as a Witch, spirit is probably the one that you will call upon the most, whether you realize it or not.

Magickal Must-Haves:
"Earth to Witch ..."

Wherever you live, it is a good idea to have someplace where you can go to get back in touch with Mother Earth. This can be as simple as sitting under a tree in your backyard or going to the beach. Even a park will do if you live in the city. The important thing is to occasionally sit your butt directly on the earth and tune in to that grounding energy.

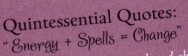

Quintessential Quotes:
"Energy + Spells = Change"

When our own energy is concentrated and channeled, it can move the broader energy currents. The images and objects used in spells are the channels, the vessels through which our power is poured and by which it is shaped. When energy is directed into the images we visualize, it gradually manifests physical form and takes shape in the material world.

—Starhawk, *The Spiral Dance*

Magic the Cat's Simple Spells:
"Energy Visualization"

Witches use energy to power their lives and their spells. Here is a simple spell to help you visualize the energy you need:

Sit in front of a candle or out in the moonlight. Close your eyes and see a core of light form in the center of your body, then slowly expand to cover your entire body. When you see yourself completely surrounded by light, say the following:

> *As above*
> *So below.*
> *I am energy*
> *Head to toe.*

faeries

feasts

familiars

FAERIES

Are there really any such things as faeries? Many Witches believe in them whole-heartedly. Others are convinced that they don't exist except in stories told to children. So are there indeed faeries at the bottom of your garden?

To be honest, I tend to lean toward the dubious group on this one…or at least I doubt that faeries look or act much like our ideas of them. On the other hand, there are a whole lot of things that I didn't think were real until I found the witchy life many years ago, so I try to keep an open mind.

Let's face it—there are many more things that we *don't* know for certain about this fabulous universe that we live in than those we do.

So let's just assume for a moment that the "yes, Virginia, there really are faeries" bunch are right—now what?

Well, for one thing, it is a good idea to play nice with the little people. After all, you can't see them, and they can see you. And if they *are* around, they have been with us for a very long time. And they were probably there before us.

So why not put out the occasional treat for them, and plant a few extra pretty flowers in the garden with them in mind. Whenever my group gets together for a ritual outside, we always leave the last few "cakes" from our cakes and ale for the faeries…just because.

And maybe when you plant your seeds down there at the bottom of your garden, it might not be a bad idea to ask the faeries for a little boost. Who knows, you might just get it!

Helpful Hints:
"Faerie Nice"

To keep the faeries in your yard happy, plant some colorful and sweet-smell-
ing flowers, and occasionally put out a treat like a bowl of milk or mead, a few
cookies, or a sparkly bauble. Be nice to them, and they'll be nice to you!

FEASTS

Ah, feasting. Did I mention that this is one of my favorite witchy activities? Of course, feasting
is not limited to the Pagan community. Even the local Methodist ladies' pot luck dinner can be
considered a feast of sorts (if you like Jell-O molds and fourteen varieties of pasta salad).

But Witches do it with style. And enthusiasm. You haven't lived until you have been to a
Beltane or Lammas feast.

Part of the fun, of course, is being with a bunch of other Witches. In many ways, the food
itself is secondary to the pleasure of simply being in a room (or a field) with a bunch of people
who believe the things that you do—not always a common occurrence if you are of the Pagan
persuasion.

The energy after a ritual is usually intense and joyful, too, which increases the appetite and
makes everything taste better (especially if you're eating outdoors and the weather is good).

Or maybe it is the love and passion that witchy folks put into making the food they bring to
feasts; or the funky, unpredictable variety of dishes made by folks who tend toward the unusual
by their very natures. I don't know.

No matter what the reason, the food at feasts is usually wonderful. (Okay, let's admit it—Pagans tend to be a bunch of hedonists—we just love to eat good food and drink good drinks!) And the sharing of food—breaking bread together—is one of the oldest traditions in the world.

So when the next witchy holiday rolls around, why not invite folks to stay for a feast after the ritual? Tell everyone to bring something fun and indulgent and maybe just a little bit extravagant (chocolate fountain, anyone?). Lift a goblet to the goddess and the god, then eat, drink, and be merry. Remember, there are no calories in food eaten at feasts with friends!

Familiars

All right, every Witch out there who has at least one cat or dog, raise your hand. Hmm…maybe it would be easier to have the ones *without* pets raise their hands instead.

The truth is, most of us have some sort of four-footed companion who shares our lives, our homes, and often our beds. (And in case of the more spoiled ones, our food and pretty much whatever else they want.)

I have to admit that I have one or two cats myself. Okay, five. (Five is close to two. Kind of.) Magic, Mystic, Minerva, Samhain, and Angus Mac (named after both an obscure Celtic god and McGyver of television fame—don't ask) are all pretty magickal in their own furry ways, of course, but in reality, it is Magic who is the most magickal.

What can I say; you've got to be careful when naming cats.

It is Magic who shows up whenever my group has a ritual, walking around the circle to greet each person in turn. When she is done with that, she either sits under the table we use for an altar or picks a perch where she can relax and supervise. She also has a thing for sage smudge sticks (go figure).

So is Magic truly magick? I'd have to say that she certainly seems to be more in tune with the energies of ritual than all the other cats, although one or the other of them will sometimes put in an appearance if they are in the mood.

In the old days, she would have been called my familiar.

Familiars were animals who were said to contain a supernatural spirit that communed with and aided their chosen Witch.

I'm not sure that Magic is any more supernatural than any other cat, but I have certainly seen in her and other animals belonging to Witches (and not just cats) that spark of something extra…a little something that I can't explain.

So if you have an animal that shares your home and your rituals, and seems to know things that an animal usually wouldn't know…feel free to call it a familiar, and I for one won't argue. And neither, I think, would Magic.

Ask Magic the Cat:
"Familiar Quandary"

Dear Magic the Cat,

I heard my Witch say that she wanted to lose weight, so I ate her dinner when she was out of the room. Now she's mad at me, and I don't know why. What's a familiar to do?

Full Fluffy in Fargo

Dear Full,

This misunderstanding was not your fault. Witches should know that when they put a request out into the universe, it may manifest in ways they didn't expect! She said she wanted to lose weight, and as long as you are snitching her food she's sure to do that—or else she'll learn not to leave food out where you can get it, in which case you will have helped to educate her. Either way, you're doing a great job as a familiar. And don't worry about her being mad at you—just give her the "sweet kitty eyes" look, and she'll be putty in your paws.

Familiarly,
Magic the Cat

Stoned!
"Fluorite Fascination"

Fluorite is a stone that is fairly new to magickal use. It comes in various combinations of clear, green, and purple, often with stripes of deep amethyst-like color. But that description doesn't do it justice; a good piece of fluorite can be the most gorgeous stone you have ever seen. It even looks spiritual, like a shard of enchanted sea frozen in time.

Fluorite is used for spells or charms involving mental powers or the conscious mind. It can be calming and soothing, easing anger so that you can think straight. It can also be useful for magickal work to ease depression or any other emotions that interfere with a clear mind—the perfect stone for today's busy Witch.

Great Gods!
"Full Moon Females"

There are many moon goddesses, including Diana, Hecate, Luna, Selene, Hathor, Isis, Artemis, Demeter, and Gaia—some of whom doubled as earth goddesses as well. They are goddesses, after all; why *shouldn't* they be able to multi-task?

As Witches, we tend to be drawn to moon goddesses, and many Witches have one in particular whom they invoke on most full moons. Do you?

So the next time the full moon rises in the sky above you, why not try this invocation:

Hail, Diana, lady of the moon!
I, _____, greet thee and honor thee!
Shine thy blessed light upon me,
and share with me the gifts of inspiration and love.
So mote it be.

garb

goddess

god

Green Man

grounding
and centering

Great Rite

G

GARB

When my group sends out invitations to our major rituals, we always include the following phrase: PLEASE WEAR GARB IF POSSIBLE. So what is garb, and why do we care if anyone wears it? I'll tell you.

Garb is the term we use to describe all sorts of witchy attire. For some, garb is as simple as a white robe; for others, it is a silk-lined, hooded cloak or a flowy dress. I have all kinds of garb. Some of it can be worn out in the mundane world, like the peasant blouses with long, romantic sleeves or the funky hippy skirts. Some of it is more ornate and only suitable for pulling out of the broom closet when I know that I will be surrounded by other Witches wearing their own magickal clothes.

I do, in fact, have a (polyester) lined, hooded cloak that I made for myself soon after I started attending rituals. I'm not the world's best seamstress, so the hem may be a little bit uneven (hey, you're not supposed to be down there anyway), but I felt it was important for me to make that particular piece of garb with my own two hands.

Garb can be made at home (uneven hems and all—heck, we're Witches, what do we care about hems?) or bought at Pagan stores or online. If you are lucky enough to get to a Renaissance fair, you will probably find some pretty amazing outfits (and if you can afford them, you're even luckier).

Or you can find "regular" clothes like the ones I described above and just call them garb. The important thing is that you are wearing something different than what you wear to go to work or to the grocery store.

And *that*, my witchy pals, is why we ask folks to wear garb to rituals.

When we change into special clothing, it reminds us that we are leaving the mundane world and entering a magickal realm outside of our everyday lives. Garb helps put us in the mood to do magick, shows respect to the gods and to each other, and serves as a symbol of who and what we are.

Of course, it doesn't hurt that it is fun to wear and makes us look really, really cool. Why do you think I have so much of it?

GODDESS

One of the things that sets Paganism apart from most of the other religions in the world is our belief in not just a patriarchal male god but in a matriarchal goddess as well. Father and mother, if you will.

As a nature-based religion, it makes sense to follow the patterns that we see everywhere in nature: male and female, that is, not just one or the other or neither (unless you're an amoeba).

The goddess we worship comes in all shapes, sizes, and colors, and we call her by various names, depending on our personal preferences or the needs of the occasion. There is even a common goddess chant that merely repeats the names of some of the most well known: Isis, Astarte, Diana, Hecate, Demeter, Kali, Inanna.

As you can see by this list, our goddesses are drawn from many cultures, including Greek, Roman, Celtic, Indian, Egyptian, and Sumerian. Does anyone know where Sumeria was, by the way? I certainly don't. Many times, the goddesses we call upon have actually outlived the culture that spawned them. Now that's immortality.

The goddess is generally known in three forms: maiden, mother, and crone, collectively referred to as the triple goddess. She changes shape as the year changes: young in the spring, middle-aged in the late summer, old in the winter, and young again as spring returns.

Most Pagans find one or more goddesses who appeal to them in particular (or who speak to them in an especially loud voice—sometimes the goddess picks you, and not the other way around) and call on her most often. Some just say "goddess" without feeling the need to attach a name. Either way, our belief in the goddess strengthens our connection to the female in all of us (yes, guys too) and to the duality in the natural world that surrounds us.

No matter what name you call the goddess or goddesses you worship, remember to treat her with respect and a bit of caution as well. These are powerful, many-faceted deities, after all. Even the lovely Venus, goddess of love and beauty, was known for her twisted sense of humor on occasion. Ever have a bad blind date? Yup, that's her, too.

Quintessential Quotes:
"Great Goddess"

The Goddess is first of all earth; the dark, nurturing mother who brings forth all life. She is the power of fertility and generation; the womb, and also the receptive tomb, the power of death. All proceeds from her; all returns to her.

—Starhawk, *The Spiral Dance*

Charmed, I'm Sure:
"Goddess Charm"

If you don't feel comfortable wearing a pentacle necklace—because you're still in the broom closet or maybe you just don't like jewelry—you can always make this goddess charm and wear or carry it instead.

Take a small white pouch (it can be leather, silk, or cotton), and place into it a piece of moonstone, a bit of vervain if you have some, and a bead or symbol that is shaped like a crescent moon. You can even just draw a moon on a slip of paper if you'd rather. Then consecrate the charm to stand as your symbol of the goddess and slip it into a purse or pocket, or around your neck. May the goddess always be with you.

GOD

Witchy practices often focus on the goddess, especially during lunar rituals such as full moon and new moon. But let us not forget her consort, the god, the masculine half of the deity. Like the goddess, the god comes in many different forms, with many different names, and he changes shape throughout the course of the year.

We draw on the same mythological pantheons for the names we call the gods as we do for our goddesses. Greek and Roman gods are often well known (Neptune, Saturn, Pluto, Mars, and Mercury ... now where have I heard those before?), as are some Celtic, Norse, and Egyptian gods (among others). Even the names of the days of the week come from the names of Norse gods, such as Thor (Thor's day became Thursday) and Woden (Wednesday).

Zeus was the father of the Greek gods and ruled from high atop Mount Olympus. (And when they say he was the father of the gods, they aren't kidding—the guy seriously got around.) The modern-day Olympics are based on a Greek festival that was held in his honor.

Jupiter was Zeus's Roman counterpart, and like Zeus, he was known for throwing thunderbolts at those who pissed him off. This was true of Thor as well, who was a god of justice. I guess you can figure out what happened to those who didn't play nice... (ouch, sizzle).

Many Witches like to call on gods from the Celtic pantheon, especially Cernunnos and Herne, both of whom were usually depicted as the figure of a man with stag's antlers. It is likely that these gods were the origin, at least in part, of the Green Man and Horned God that play such an important part in Pagan worship. We also call on the sun god Lugh, especially on Lughnasadh, the holiday we celebrate in his honor.

Apollo was the Greek sun god who was also a god of healing. Traditionally, the sun tended to be the domain of the gods, while the moon fell under the influence of the goddess. This may explain why the god dies during the darkest time of the year and then is reborn at Yule, when the light is beginning to return.

As with the goddess, some Witches call the god by one particular name, or many, or simply use "the god." It is worth taking the time to explore the many myths and stories surrounding the Pagan gods. Not only are the stories interesting in their own right, but you never know when some god will pop out and call your name, informing you that from that time on, you may call him—and he will answer.

Green Man

The Green Man is a common Pagan symbol that originated on the British Isles. With the face of a man surrounded by leaves (usually oak), the Green Man is often pictured with horns, which may have led to his mistaken identification by some as a Satanic figure.

On the contrary, the Green Man represents life in the form of trees and other plants. He was a popular figure in medieval art and can be found carved on old churches all over Europe.

Also known as "Green Jack" or "Jack-in-the-Green," the Green Man is the representative of the spirits that live in all growing things.

The Green Man is a god of the woods and therefore associated with all the creatures that might be found there, including woodland faeries. (You laugh? Well, try *not* including them, and see where that gets you.)

As a god who brought rain and encouraged growth in the fields, he was directly responsible for the survival of those long-ago Pagans who lived off the land. Even today you can often find Green Man carvings that are designed to be placed in the garden to encourage plants to grow and flourish.

Green Man figures may be carved out of wood or cast from plaster or metal; they may be large or small, meant to be used indoors or out. However he is depicted, the Green Man is symbolic of our roots as a nature-based religion and as such deserves a place of honor in every Pagan home.

GROUNDING AND CENTERING

If you look at almost every ritual, you will at some point find an instruction that tells you to "ground and center." For instance, you may be told to drum to raise energy, send that energy into your spell, then ground and center. No problem, right?

Except for one thing: hardly anybody actually tells you how to do it. Maybe Witches are supposed to be born knowing how to ground and center? But just in case you don't know, here are some simple suggestions:

There are really two different kinds of grounding and centering, and we do them for two completely different reasons. (Yeah, I know, many of the books don't mention that either. So pay attention.)

The first is when we start a ritual and need to focus on what we will be doing. In this case, grounding and centering serves to give us the strength for the task ahead and helps us to shut out distractions so that we can give all our attention to the magickal work.

The second is toward the end of a ritual, as in the example above, when we have built up all sorts of magickal energy and sent it into our magick. In this case, grounding and centering serves to channel any remaining "excess" energy out of us and into the ground. If you don't do this step, you will probably be up all night, buzzing and humming and bouncing off the walls. (Which, while amusing for those around you, can be kind of unpleasant.)

You can use the same techniques for both types of G & C. The simplest method is to close your eyes, take three slow, deep breaths, and feel your body connect to the earth below you. If you are doing G & C at the end of a ritual, sometimes it helps to put both your hands flat on the ground (or floor, if you're inside—the ground is still under there somewhere) and visualize the energy moving down into the earth.

If you need something more powerful, say to ground yourself before a ritual if you are frazzled or upset, then try this exercise:

Start with the three slow, deep breaths, then visualize yourself as a tree. (What? Oh, any kind of tree, it doesn't matter.) See your roots coming out of your feet and growing slowly downward, getting larger and stronger as they go. Take however long you need to do this, then see your branches spreading up toward the sky. If it helps, you can lift up your arms. Feel the energy of the sun coming down to meet the energy of the earth as it moves up, and visualize them meeting in your center as a ball of glowing light. Take another few deep breaths and then channel that light and power into your magick.

And that, my friends, is how you ground and center.

What is the Great Rite, and what is so great about it, anyway? Well, there's sex involved, if that gives you any idea.

The Great Rite is the name for the traditional ritual in which the high priestess and high priest of a coven are joined together sexually to symbolize the joining of the god and the goddess. Yup, right there in front of everybody.

But don't get the wrong impression. This is a sacred rite, and–when done correctly—it is intended as an act of worship, not simply an act of sex. Traditionally, the Great Rite was enacted at sabbats, most especially at Samhain as a reaffirmation of life in the midst of the coming darkness and at Beltane as a celebration of the return of life and light.

To be honest, I'm not sure how much the Great Rite is used anymore, at least in its original form. It is something that is done mostly in Gardnerian-type covens, and I have never been a member of one, so I don't know. These days, Witches are more likely to enact the Great Rite symbolically, by putting an athame into a chalice at the close of ritual. (The athame represents the male, or god, and the chalice represents the female, or goddess.)

What I do know is that if you are lucky enough to be part of a Pagan couple, you and your honey can enact the Great Rite on your own, and invite the god and goddess into your own sacred ritual. Now *that* would be a great rite, indeed.

Food of the Gods:
"Garlic"

Garlic is a powerful herb (and I'm not just talking about the smell). It can be used magickally for protection and exorcism (should you have a need for such a thing) and medicinally for pretty much the same thing.

It is considered to be a surety against drowning and is used in most protection charms. One subtle way to utilize garlic for protection is to hang up a garlic braid in your kitchen. Decorative and useful at the same time, and no one will know you're doing magick.

But mostly it is just darned tasty. Use it in anything Italian, in soups, and as a spread on freshly baked bread. And don't worry about your breath…at least it will scare away the vampires!

Witch 101:
"It's Easy Being Green"

Some Witches call themselves Green Witches—this refers not only to the witchy connection with the earth and ecology but to a particular type of practice. Green Witches often base their practice on Celtic traditions and sometimes focus part of their work on a connection with the faery world. For a great book on the subject, check out *Green Witchcraft: Folk Magic, Fairy Lore & Herb Craft* by Ann Moura (Aoumiel).

herbs

history

high priestess/
high priest

Hecate

healing

H

Herbs

Herbs may be a Witch's best friend. They are easy to grow (think weeds) and can often be nurtured in as small a space as a windowsill or a table-top pot. Many herbs that have magickal properties can be used for culinary and healing purposes as well. Most of them smell wonderful, and many of them have beautiful flowers, too. What's not to like?

Of course, a few of the more commonly used magickal herbs are deadly poisons...but nobody's perfect. Just be sure that you do your research, and keep any dangerous herbs away from children and pets. (And if something is called deadly nightshade, you might take that as a hint.)

Herbs have been used by Pagans for magick and medicine since the dawn of time. Dried herbs have been found buried with the pharaohs in Egyptian tombs, and the ancient Druids were known for their skill with plants. The wise women in European villages used herbs to cure everything from coughs to warts and sold charm bags to lovers on the side. Native Americans are justly famous for their herbal wisdom.

If you live in the country, you probably want to have a sizable chunk of your garden set aside for herbs such as basil, bergamot, calendula, chamomile, comfrey, dill, garlic, lavender, lemon balm, nettle, parsley, peppermint, rosemary, rue, sage, spearmint, thyme, valerian, vervain, and yarrow. Many of these can be used in prosperity, love, or protection magick as well as for cooking and healing work. (Do your research before eating, though, and remember that even the grooviest magickal herbs can still make you sneeze if you're allergic to them.)

But what do you do if you're a city Witch or live in an apartment with no place to put a garden because your landlord uses the backyard for biker get-togethers and as a place to chain his pit bulls?

Not to worry. Not only can you grow a few of your favorite herbs in a sunny corner of your city loft (and I do recommend doing that for the fun of it, if nothing else), but many herbs are readily available at the grocery store (fresh only; never buy the dried ones there, as they are often too old, treated with crap, or otherwise unsuitable), the health food store, a local farmer's market, or by mail order. You can get magickal herbs in particular from many Pagan and New Age sources, often already made up into oils, charms, potions, or other useful, witchy forms.

But don't forget to make up your own charms and such from time to time. It may be easier to buy them ready-made, but each stage of the process—planting, growing, harvesting, and preparing—is infused with your energy and your intent, so that the end result is more powerful, more magickal, and more connected to you. And that is what being a Witch is all about.

Magickal Must-Haves:
"Herbal Handbooks"

Most Witches work with herbs a lot. It is important to have good sources for accurate information, and these are some of the best: Scott Cunningham's *Magical Herbalism* and *Encyclopedia of Magical Herbs* (along with his *Encyclopedia of Wicca in the Kitchen*), Sally Dubats' *Natural Magick: The Essential Witch's Grimoire,* and Gerina Dunwich's *Wicca Garden: A Modern Witch's Book of Magickal and Enchanted Herbs and Plants*. There are many more, but these are the ones I tend to grab when I am looking for the perfect herb for a spell or info for whichever book I happen to be working on at the time.

HISTORY

I have never been much of a history buff. I hate to say it, but I could never keep the kings of England straight (King Henry the Fifth, King George the Second—I'll bet even their mothers got confused). I don't remember the date that the Magna Carta was signed, and I could probably only tell you the names of about half the presidents of the United States (although I *can* tell you the name of the woman that Captain Kirk fell in love with when he traveled back through time, if that would be of any help...)

But since I became a Pagan, I have developed a new interest in history, in part because I have discovered how much of what is so-called common knowledge is just plain wrong, and how much I didn't know about the history of Paganism in particular.

I have learned all sorts of interesting facts, from the trivial to the important. Did you know, for instance, that the word *Pagan* means "country dweller" and only became a name for the followers of the Old Religion after Christianity took hold in the courts of kings and the big cities of the time, and the only hold-outs were those who lived in the far-flung rural areas? (Needless to say, the word was not used as a compliment.)

Or that when King James (don't ask me which number) had the Bible translated into the version that is still in common use today, the meanings of a number of words were changed to fit the political climate of the time—so the passage everyone quotes that says "thou shalt not suffer a Witch to live" used to say "evil sorceress" in the original Hebrew. Makes kind of a difference, doesn't it?

There are also the truly unpleasant parts of Pagan history, of course—the years known as the Burning Times, when Witches were hunted and killed and much of our precious knowledge was lost forever; the political maneuvers and power struggles that resulted in the loss of freedom for women and created systematic lies about Witches that are still believed by the majority of non-Pagans because they have never learned differently.

These too are part of our history.

I believe that it is more important than ever for Pagans to learn about our own special place in history. Not just so that we know the facts, although that is important in and of itself, but so that we can share these facts with our non-Pagan friends and family and anyone else that we can get to listen.

If we are to write a new chapter in the book of Paganism, one with a happier ending, we must know the beginning of the story and tell it to the world. Only in this way can we leave a different history for our children and for all the generations of Pagans yet to come.

Required Reading:
"History Lessons"

If you want to get into more depth on the history of Witchcraft, here are a couple of books that were recommended to me by my circle-sister Robin. She said that both are inspiring and interesting, although she warns that the second book contains some controversial topics. Read them yourself, and see what you think:

Witches and Neighbors: The Social and Cultural Context of European Witchcraft by Robin Briggs (Penguin, 1998)

The Witch in History: Early Modern and Twentieth-Century Representations by Diane Purkiss (Routledge, 1996)

HIGH PRIESTESS/HIGH PRIEST

I am a Wiccan high priestess. Is this a big deal? Well, yes and no.

One of the unique aspects of the Pagan world is that all Witches are, on some level at least, priests and priestesses. Unlike many other religions where it is necessary to have someone "official" to talk to god for you, in Paganism we are all equally capable of speaking to our deity and being heard. What can I say? There is no Pagan pope.

There are, however, high priests and high priestesses. So what makes these folks any different than the Solitary Witch who worships alone at his or her altar? On many levels, not a darned thing. To a very great extent, all Witches are the same (spiritually speaking, that is).

On the other hand, there are some Pagans who have more experience, more wisdom, or more aptitude for leadership. These Witches often end up leading a group and taking on a more open role in the wider community. Some of them even write a nifty book or two...

Traditionally, Witches met in groups led by both a high priest and a high priestess. These staunch souls would lead rituals and pass on their knowledge and eventually designate others to do the same with groups of their own. (I talked a bit about this in the coven section, which I am sure you read carefully and memorized for the quiz.)

These days, we still have high priests and high priestesses, and they still lead and pass on what they know. But they are less likely to run their groups in as formal (or secretive) a manner. They may have trained and studied for years under an older and wiser Witch (as I was fortunate enough to be able to do) or they may be self-taught.

Either way, I believe that it is still important for our community to have leaders (someone needs to organize the feast!) and people who are responsible for the passing down of our lore, facts, and fancies to the next generation.

So yes, in some ways, it is a big deal. As long as I remember to get someone to bring the dessert.

Wit from the World Wide Web:
"The Priest, the Rabbi, and the Pagan Priestess"

As part of an interfaith community project, a right-wing Christian priest, a rabbi, and a Pagan priestess decided that in order to improve relations in the community, they will go on a fishing trip together on a local pond.

They're out in the boat, and the Pagan priestess excuses herself to go to the bathroom back on the shore. She gets out, walks across the water back to the shore, and then walks back across the water to the boat.

The Christian priest looks in amazement, crosses himself, and they continue fishing. It comes on about noontime, and the rabbi realizes they left their lunches back on shore. So he gets up, walks across the water to the shore, retrieves the lunches, and walks back across the water to the boat.

The Christian priest, now completely amazed and a little bit righteous, thinks *not to be outdone by two heathens, I can do that too!* So he gets up, excuses himself to go to the bathroom, takes a step out of the boat, and promptly sinks to the bottom.

While he's flailing around in the water, the rabbi looks at the priestess and says, "Do you think we should have told him about the rocks?"

The Pagan priestess replies, "What rocks?"[6]

---

6 From http:/www.bewitchingways.com/humor/rocks.htm (accessed 31 May 2007).

HECATE

My personal favorite goddess is Hecate, the patron goddess of Witches. Hecate is found in the Celtic pantheon, and her origins can be traced back to the Greek Hekate. Like many of the goddesses, Hecate is a triple goddess, appearing in different forms at different times. She has three aspects: goddess of fertility, goddess of the moon, and goddess of the night. In her aspect as dark goddess, she is often pictured wearing a necklace of testicles, with hair made of snakes. (What can I say? The lady has a serious dark side.)

As with much in the Pagan belief system, Hecate is both light and dark, giving life and taking it away. To quote *The Element Encyclopedia of Witchcraft,* "Hecate holds dominion over life, death, regeneration and magic. She rules wisdom, choices, expiation, victory, vengeance and travel."[7] In other words, she's one powerful Queen of the Night. Do not mess with her.

Hecate is often pictured with hounds, as the dog is one of her sacred animals. Her sacred place was the crossroads, especially where three roads met, and she is celebrated at the dark moon, unlike most of her full moon sister-goddesses. Her symbols are the key, the cauldron, the broom, and the torch, and her plants are garlic, lavender, and mandrake.

Hecate guards the border between life and death but also officiates at births and watches over women and children. Perhaps what draws me to her the most is this balancing between the light and the dark, the physical and the spiritual. She seems to me to embody the essence of what Witchcraft is—mysterious and beautiful, capable of great acts of kindness but shadowed with darkness. As human beings, we are wonderful but often flawed; I'm sure that the Queen of Witches understands that and loves us anyway.

---

7   Illes, 386.

Ask Magic the Cat:
"Horned God Who?"

Dear Magic the Cat,

I am a Witch with lots of animals: I have two dogs, three cats, and a corn snake named Sarah. Can you tell me if there is a god or goddess that is best for an animal lover like me to invoke for magick to help my pets?

Barnyard Babe in Bristol

Dear Babe,

You sound like my kind of Witch! (The snake stays in her terrarium, right?) There are many gods and goddesses who are associated with animals. A few of my favorite animal-rights gods are the Horned God (who is sacred to wild animals in particular), Artemis (who protects animals), Bast (cat goddess—my favorite, of course!), Hecate (who likes both dogs and snakes, although I'm not sure why), Diana, and Cernunnos. Of course, most of the gods look kindly on the occasional sacrifice ... I hear that canned cat food works very well.

Familiarly,
Magic the Cat

HEALING

As Witches, we do magickal work for various reasons: prosperity, love, luck, power, and all that good stuff. But maybe the most important magick we do is healing magick.

Healing magick can be done in numerous ways—anything from a simple spell to a magickal bath to a healing charm to an herbal tea spiced up with a little magickal boost. As with all other magick, the most important component is your intent; other than that, you can choose whichever method seems most appropriate for the problem at hand.

Magickal healing work can be done not only for physical healing but also for emotional, psychological, and psychic healing as well. My group once did a family healing spell when a couple of members were having difficulties dealing with parents, husbands, and children. It worked, too.

Healing work is best done on a Sunday or a Monday, when the moon is waxing to full (to increase health). If you need to work during the waning moon, then you can try doing magick to decrease illness instead. If you are using color and/or candle magick, try blue (for healing and peace) or green (for healing and growth). If working to banish illness, then black works well.

Many stones can be used in magickal work as well: clear quartz crystals, amethyst, lapis, and bloodstone are among the best. Some people even use one stone for each color of the chakras and place them on the appropriate spot on the body.

One important point about healing magick: if you are going to do it for someone else, you must—I repeat, *must*—get permission first. Witches believe in free will, and I cannot stress enough how important that concept is to the core of being a Witch. It is not up to you to decide if someone should be ill or not; each individual is entitled to make that decision for themselves.

So by all means, do healing magick for someone if they ask you to, but otherwise, the most that you can do is send a heartfelt prayer to the gods that everything will turn out in the best possible way—and be prepared to accept that sometimes "the best possible way" isn't what you would have chosen.

Magic the Cat's Simple Spells:
"Down the Drain Healing"

All herbs with healing qualities will work in magick, but my Witch is particularly fond of eucalyptus, rosemary, and lemon balm. She suggests taking a bath with a few herbs (essential oils work as well) and some sea salt, to draw out negativity and other bad stuff. To make it work even better, sit in the tub as the water runs out, and visualize your symptoms going down the drain with it. Sometimes the most powerful magickal work is also the simplest. Of course, if you were a cat, you'd never have to take a bath at all…

Stoned!
"Hematite Healing"

Hematite is an unusually heavy, silvery black gemstone that is primarily used for healing, grounding, and divination. You can hold it in your hands in front of a problem area and visualize it drawing the illness from your body. (Be sure to cleanse the stone afterwards—nobody likes a piece of hematite with germs!) If you have a big enough piece, you can also use it for scrying.

Hematite makes great jewelry and pairs well with black onyx (another grounding stone) and carnelian (for healing). If you are someone who is always in need of grounding, a simple hematite band worn on your dominant hand might help.

Just be aware that in the good old days, the stone that we now know as bloodstone was often referred to as hematite (no, I don't know why—it just was, that's all), so if you come across old magickal references to hematite, they probably don't mean the stone we use today.

Ask Onyx:
"Happiness Is a Witch"

Dear Onyx,

I have been having a really hard time lately, and I have tried doing magick to bring happiness into my life, but it's not working. What am I doing wrong?

Hopeless in Hoboken

Dear Hopeless,

Doing magick to bring happiness into your life is a good start, but it is only the first step. Remember that when working magick, we also have to do the necessary work in the "real world" to help bring our magick to fruition. So what are you doing to change whatever is in your life that is making you unhappy to start out with? Try to be more specific about the problem—do you want a different job, more friends, for your boyfriend to treat you better? Then you can work more specific magick and maybe figure out what *you* need to do to change your life for the better. Sometimes it is as simple as having more reasonable expectations of what "happiness" really means to you ...

Bright blessings,
Onyx

Elemental Essentials:
"Handfastings"

Handfastings are Pagan wedding ceremonies. These can be legal (if performed by a high priestess/high priest who is also an ordained minister) or solely religious ceremonies. They can be done for "a year and a day" (a common Pagan period of time) or for life, and (unlike standard legal ceremonies in most areas) handfastings may be performed between same-sex couples as well as more traditional pairs. The only true essential element here is love and a shared sense of commitment.

ignorance

invocation

Imbolc

Isis

IGNORANCE

One of my favorite jokes goes like this: What is the difference between ignorance and apathy? Answer: I don't know and I don't care.

Pretty funny, but in real life ignorance is no laughing matter—especially when you are on the receiving end of religious bigotry that is based on misinformation or no information at all. And, alas, there's a lot of that out there.

So what's a Witch to do?

Sadly, for many Witches, the harsh realities of a predominantly ignorant world make staying in the broom closet a necessity. If you are a Pagan working in a conservative rural school system, for instance, it is probably not a great idea to go around shouting "I'm a Witch" at parent-teacher conferences. (Although I can see the temptation...)

This makes it even more important for those of us who *can* come out of the broom closet to do so and to present ourselves to the community at large in a manner that reflects well on all Witches.

For while it is true that there is a lot of ignorance out there, to some extent that is our own fault. We Witches have gotten so used to hiding who and what we are that most people don't have a clue as to how many of us are out there, what it means to be a Pagan, or how much we contribute to society.

And while it is also true that living openly as Witches may subject us to prejudice, negative comments, and even legal difficulties (especially when it comes to child custody battles), we are fortunate enough to live in a time when secrecy is no longer a matter of life and death.

Each of us has to make the decision for ourselves whom to tell and when, and whether or not to come out of that musty old broom closet. But I believe that until many more of us choose to lead our lives openly as Witches, this state of ignorance will continue to exist, and we will have no one to blame but ourselves.

If we want them to know, we have to care.

So if you can, do a little bit to roll back the curtain of secrecy that has hidden us for so long from the eyes of our neighbors. Start with your friends and family, move on to those you work with and live near, and go from there. You might be surprised at how many people are willing to learn more about us if you give them a chance.

And if you are out there in the open, remember that in some ways you are representing all Witches. So stand up straight, wear your funky clothes with pride, and try not to scare the neighbors on Samhain (much).

INVOCATION

Our old pal Webster defines invocation as the act or process of petitioning for help or support, a prayer of entreaty (as at the beginning of a service of worship), or a formula for conjuring. Maybe Webster was a Witch?

Well, okay, probably not. But these are all pretty good descriptions of what an invocation is in the magickal world.

Specifically, there are two kinds of invocations that are almost always used in Pagan rituals. The first is what we usually refer to as "calling the quarters."

The other common form of invocation that we use in rituals is somewhat different. After we summon the quarters, we invoke the goddess and the god, or sometimes just one or the other—for instance, on full moons we often only call on the goddess. The main difference here is that while we *summon* the elements, we *ask* the gods to join us in our circle. (Politely, if we know what's good for us.)

After all, they are gods and we are just puny mortals. There is no way that we can order them to do anything.

So we *ask* them to come to our circles. Nicely. God and goddess invocations are essentially a way of getting their attention and letting them know that we would like very much for them to spend some time with us, pretty please.

A typical goddess invocation used for a full moon ritual might go something like this:

Great Goddess, mother of us all, we ask you to join us here in our circle as we
celebrate this, your night. Under the glowing moon, we gather in your name and seek
to use the power that you have given us. We ask you to join us and aid us in our task.
Welcome, and blessed be.

It is important to be respectful in both kinds of invocations (since the elements are our allies, not our servants) but especially when calling upon the gods. It just makes sense. After all, you wouldn't call up your parents and order them to come to dinner, even if that tactic actually worked on your younger brother.

You will note that the last definition of invocation is "a formula for conjuring." Technically, this would mean that any spell or incantation is also an invocation. And you can certainly call

Quintessential Quotes:
" Invocation"

In some ways this is the heart of all Wiccan ritual,
and indeed is the only necessary part. Wiccan rites
are attunements with the powers that are the
Goddess and God; all else is pageantry.
—Scott Cunningham, *Wicca*

them that if you want to; the Pagan Definition Police will probably not show up at your house and haul you away. (This time.) But in general, when we use the term *invocation* in magick, we are talking about calling the quarters or the gods, not casting a spell.

IMBOLC

Imbolc is what's known as a cross-quarter holiday, and it falls on February 2, midway between Yule and Ostara. If that date seems familiar to you, it is because these days it is known to most folks (the non-witchy kind, anyway) as Groundhog Day. Whatever you call it, Imbolc celebrates the first signs of spring and the end of winter's cold and gloom. Admittedly, in some parts of the country, such as my home in upstate New York, you kind of have to take the "spring is coming" bit on faith, but it is still worth celebrating all the same.

Imbolc was originally a Celtic holiday dedicated to Brigit, the goddess of smithcraft, healing, and the arts. It is also a fire festival, so it is well suited for bonfires, lots of candles, and anything creative in nature. Try having a Pagan poetry reading, or maybe a sacred s'mores party (hey, any excuse for chocolate).

For Witches, this is a time of cleansing and purification as we ready ourselves to enter the more active part of the year. The goddess is a maiden again, and the young god—reborn at Yule—is moving from infancy into robust childhood. The earth is shaking off her wintry sleep and rousing herself in preparation for another season of growth and renewal, which makes it the perfect time for us to do the same.

If you want, try taking a ritual cleansing bath on Imbolc Eve. Put a few drops of lavender oil in the tub along with some sea salt, light a few candles, and listen to some soothing music. (Note: the candles should go near the tub, not in the tub. Just so we're clear.) While you sit in the bath, feel the warm water washing away the stresses and negativity of the winter season, and visualize yourself rising like Venus out of the ocean (or Neptune, if you're a guy)—powerful, energized, and ready to face the challenges of the season ahead.

Isis

Isis is an Egyptian goddess of the moon and a mother goddess. She is also a major Witch goddess, as you can tell from her names: she is also called "Mistress of Magic," "She Who Is Rich in Spells," "Great of Sorcery," "Speaker of Spells," and "The Great Witch." Yup, she's one of ours, all right!

Isis was one of the primary deities of ancient Egypt. At the peak of her influence, she was worshipped from East Africa through western Asia and into Europe. In Rome, she stood out from other gods of the time because the cult of Isis was open to all—including slaves and (gasp!) women. (What were they thinking?)

Many of the images of Isis portray her with her son Horus, and she is identified with the virgin in the constellation of Virgo. Interestingly enough, some statues of the Madonna and baby were apparently modeled on early statues of Isis and Horus.

She fell in love with her brother/husband Osiris while they were still in their mother's womb, and together they represent the timeless love of perfect soul mates. (Okay, so marrying your brother isn't your idea of romance—picky, picky.)

To make an offering to Isis, use milk, honey, flowers, or incense. Bloodstone is her sacred stone, and vervain and myrrh are her sacred herbs. She is also associated with healing, childbirth, water, and the moon, and is often pictured as a beautiful woman crowned with a crescent moon between a ram's horns.

Isis doesn't just represent the essence of all that is witchy, she also stands for wisdom, truth, and power. So next full moon, think about pouring a little milk on the ground under the light of the stars and say a heartfelt blessed be to Isis, the lady of the moon.

In the Witch's Tool Chest:
"Incense Incidentals"

When choosing incense for a ritual, try picking one that matches your magickal goal. For instance, if you are doing magick for healing, you may wish to use an incense that contains eucalyptus, sandalwood, or lavender. On the other hand, if you are doing magick for peace, you may want bergamot or jasmine.

Many of us love incense but have problems with allergies or sensitivity to strong smells. Luckily, there are many types of incense these days that are made with completely natural ingredients (essential oils instead of perfume oils), which are less likely to irritate the sensitive. Just read labels and descriptions carefully. And if you are doing a ritual inside, remember that less is more. Whatever your personal preferences, if you are doing rituals with others, it is good etiquette to go with something mild and natural, just in case.

Witch 101:
"Inside the Internet"

One great source for information these days is the Internet. Not only can you find wonderful sites full of witchy spells and info on sabbats, esbats, and Pagan lore, but even sites that give you dates and times for local events or Pagan dating services (check out Witchvox in particular for that sort of thing nationwide). And don't forget to check out the great books at Llewellyn's website.

Keep in mind that just because it is on the Internet doesn't make it true, and use some common sense. If something doesn't sound right to you, it probably isn't.

Ask Onyx:
"Initiation vs. Dedication"

Dear Onyx,

I have some witchy friends who say they have been dedicated and some who say they have been initiated—what's the difference? And do I have to do either to practice as a Witch?

Undedicated in Utica

Dear Undedicated,

Some people use these terms more or less interchangeably, but technically speaking (if Witches can ever be said to be technical, that is), dedication is when you commit yourself to the practice of Witchcraft, either as a Solitary or in a group. The ceremony can be as simple or as complicated as you wish.

Initiation, on the other hand, is strictly a coven thing—after a certain amount of time in a group, the high priest and/or high priestess will decide that you are ready (sometimes it is a year and a day, sometimes after you have met particular goals), and then you will be formally initiated into that particular coven. And no, you don't have to do either. If you believe you are a Witch and act accordingly, that's good enough for me.

Bright blessings,
Onyx

jewelry

jasper

juniper

JEWELRY

Most Witches have a particular fondness for jewelry. I think that this is a good thing—and not just because I make jewelry for a part of my living.

Jewelry has a number of good things going for it from the witchy point of view. For instance, you can integrate various types of magickal paraphernalia into some form of wearable art: anything from a lapis bracelet to help with healing, a rune symbol to give you strength, or a necklace that holds a vial of magickal oil.

I make a number of magickal necklaces (what I call my "Spirit and Potential" line) that feature gemstones that are all especially suited for a particular use, such as healing, prosperity, love, or peace. I consecrate and bless them to make them even more powerful, but to the average person they look like no more than a pretty piece of jewelry. (Sneaky but effective.)

Many Pagans who are out of the broom closet wear a pentacle openly on a chain or cord around their necks, and even those who must be more secretive may have one tucked under their shirts where no one can see it. (You can often tell someone who is new to the Craft because they are wearing a pentacle the size of a small dinner plate. There's nothing wrong with that, of course, but most of us prefer to be a bit subtler.)

It is a rare Witch who doesn't have a favorite pentacle necklace, even if it is only worn for rituals or to other Pagan-only occasions. A lot of Witches like to wear a pentacle that incorporates other symbols of Witchcraft, like a crescent moon, oak leaves, or a Witch's broom, and many of us have pentacles that also contain a stone, like moonstone (which is sacred to the goddess) or amethyst (which can help to boost psychic ability).

Like dressing up in garb, putting on our witchy jewelry can also help to put us in the proper frame of mind for ritual work by serving as one more reminder that we are preparing ourselves to do magick.

Jewelry can also help us to identify each other when we are out and about in the mundane world. If you see someone wearing a pentacle around their neck, you can go up to them and say "merry meet," and in all likelihood they will answer you with "merry meet" or "merry part" and a great big smile!

So wear your jewelry with pride, my witchy friends, whether or not anyone else can see it. Like I always say, a decorative Witch is a happy Witch.

Quintessential Quotes:
"Jewelry"

Some people feel that jewelry has no place in the Circle. There are some who feel that it is a hindrance to the raising of power—although in almost a quarter of a century of practice I have never found this to be true. I do, however, respect those who feel this way. If they truly believe that it restricts, then it will restrict. So, decide for yourself whether to encourage the use of jewelry; whether to limit its use; whether to use it to denote position; whether to prohibit it altogether.

—Raymond Buckland, *Buckland's Complete Book of Witchcraft*

JASPER

If amethyst is the queen of gemstones—showy, beautiful, and expensive—then jasper is the guy next door. Common, dependable, and easy to find, jasper has been used in magickal work for as long as its royal purple cousin and for many of the same purposes.

Believe it or not, they really are related. Jasper is a form of chalcedony, which is a type of quartz, as is amethyst. But jasper is more than just a poor relative, and it has charms of its own for those who are willing to see.

Generally speaking, jasper is a protective stone and is especially good for protection of mother and baby during childbirth. I often use it as a component in house protection charms.

Unlike most stones that are always found in one particular color (like amethyst, which is one shade of purple or another), jasper comes in many various hues. Often its use depends on which color of jasper you have. For instance:

Red jasper is used for protection and in defensive magick (to send back whatever nasty energy some mean person has sent in your direction, no doubt through no fault of yours since you are a really nice person who would never do anything to piss anyone else off). It can also be used for health, healing, and beauty spells (not that anyone who is reading this book would need one of those).

Green jasper is used to promote health and speed healing. It is said to be helpful with insomnia and to increase empathy.

Brown jasper is good for grounding and centering (brown being the color of the element of earth, which has this quality). It is especially beneficial for people who tend to be, shall we say, a bit airy in nature.

There are a number of types of jasper that are mottled or multicolored, usually in brown, tan, red, or black combinations. Most of these work well for protection too.

In short, jasper is another stone to add to your "must-have" witchy toolkit list, but at least you won't have to mortgage your house to get it.

JUNIPER

When we talk about doing herbal magick, many Witches automatically think of garden herbs like sage and rosemary. But it is important to remember that in this context, the term *herb* also includes many common bushes, shrubs, and trees as well.

Juniper is a particularly nice magickal bush, and not just because they use juniper berries to make gin. Juniper, or *Juniperus communis* to give it its formal Latin name, has been used in magick from Egypt to Europe as well as being a favorite of the Native Americans right here at home.

It was sacred to Inanna and Ishtar, and branches from the juniper bush or tree—it can come in either form—were often burned in celebration of the gods. It is still a good choice to throw into a bonfire when you are doing magickal work outdoors (I strongly advise against bonfires inside), or you can use juniper incense no matter where you are.

Juniper is primarily used for protection, either as incense or by hanging up a sprig in a corner of your house or yard. Ironically, although it is used in this manner to ward off danger, juniper is also used to draw in love (and increase male potency—as if that isn't dangerous!).

To attract love, string some of the berries into a necklace or put them into a charm. Or burn juniper incense as part of a love-drawing ritual. But it's best not to take it internally (except as gin, of course), as it can be harmful in large amounts.

Magic the Cat's Simple Spells:
"Juniper Justice"

Here is a simple spell using juniper to protect your home from thieves and negative energy:

Cut a sprig of juniper and tie a piece of red string around it. Sprinkle it with salt and water to consecrate it, then hang it up by the front door while saying the following:

With this herb I cast this charm
And protect my home from harm.
So mote it be.

While theoretically this charm will work indefinitely, it can't hurt to replace or refresh it once a year.

Stoned!
"Jet & Amber"

Traditionally, Witch's necklaces were often made from a combination of jet and amber. Although they are usually listed with gemstones, neither of them is actually a stone. (Hah, fooled you!)

Jet is fossilized wood, and amber is fossilized resin. They are both very, very old, which may be part of their mystique. In fact, amber is said to be the oldest form of adornment worn by humans, and beads made out of the resin have been found in graves going back as far as 8000 BCE.

Amber is a clear yellowy orange, and jet is a glossy black. Together, they represent the god and the goddess, and they are reputed to increase the magickal power of the wearer. They are both used to absorb negativity and increase health.

Wit from the World Wide Web:
"Witch Jokes"

Q: What do you say to an angry Witch?

A: Ribbit.

Q: What's the best thing about Pagan friends?

A: They worship the ground you walk on.

Q: Why do Witches use brooms?

A: Because nature abhors a vacuum.

Q: What do you call 13 Witches in a hot tub?

A: A self-cleaning coven.

Q: What happens when a ceremonial magician gets angry?

A: He goes Qa-ballistic.

Q: What do you get when you cross a Zen Buddhist and a Druid?

A: Someone who worships the tree that is not there.

Q: If a Witch practices on the beach, is she a sandwich?

knots

Kitchen Witch

KNOTS

A lot of Witchcraft involves what we call sympathetic magick. No, this doesn't mean doing magick for people you feel sorry for (although that's okay, too). Sympathetic magick is when you use one thing (a poppet or doll, for instance) to represent another (the person the spell is going to affect).

Knot magick is one of the oldest and simplest forms of sympathetic magick. Its use dates back to ancient Mesopotamia, and it went on to spread through Greece, Rome, and on into the rest of Europe. Although it originated with male mystics, it eventually came to be thought of as "women's magick" because working with thread was seen as a woman's occupation. (As if woman's magick was somehow less powerful because a woman did it. Silly, I know, but there's the medieval male mind for you.)

Knot magick is a type of sympathetic magick because the knot represents binding. Essentially, you tie the knots as you cast your spell, and this action binds the power of the spell into the thread or cord you are using, making the spell more powerful and longer lasting.

You can tie just one knot or you can use the more traditional practice of using a long cord and tying nine knots, with the first knot at one end, the second at the other end, the third in the middle, the fourth and fifth halfway between the end and the middle, the sixth and seventh between the fourth and fifth and the end, and the last two between the central knot and the ones closest to it. (If this is too confusing, don't worry about it: just tie nine knots anywhere.)

Either way, remember to focus on the spell you are doing and what you are trying to achieve.

There are many variations on the words to say while you are tying the knots, and you can always just make up your own. But here is one example I particularly like:

> By the knot of one, the spell's begun.
>
> By the knot of two, it cometh true.
>
> By the knot of three, so mote it be.
>
> By the knot of four, open the door.
>
> By the knot of five, the spell's alive.
>
> By the knot of six, the spell is fixed.
>
> By the knot of seven, the stars of heaven.
>
> By the knot of eight, the stroke of fate.
>
> By the knot of nine, the thing is mine!

When you are done with your knot magick, remember to put your thread or cord on your altar or someplace else that is safe—there is a lot of power "tied" up in it now! (Sorry, I couldn't help myself.)

Helpful Hints:
"Knot Hard"

If you want to carry a spell around with you but don't want to lug around a charm bag or such, simply tie a knot into a small piece of string when you first cast the spell (this will bind the spell into the string), and tuck it into your wallet or purse.

KITCHEN WITCH

Speaking of women's magick, one of the oldest forms of Pagan witchiness was what we now call kitchen magick. Like knot magick, this was considered to be women's magick because the kitchen was women's territory. These days, of course, there are almost as many men in the kitchen as women, and kitchen magick is used by both sexes.

Traditionally, however, the kitchen was one place where women could safely work their subtle magick with a fair degree of certainty that the men around them would have no idea there was anything out of the ordinary going on. (Hee, hee, hee.)

Think of the image of a crone stirring a bubbling pot of some mysterious potion, and you'll see what I mean.

Even today there are advantages to using kitchen witchery, especially if you are a Witch who is still practicing from within the shadows of the broom closet. Most of the tools that a Kitchen Witch uses can be left out in the open and no one will be the wiser. (Magickal knife? What magickal knife?) After all, what self-respecting cook doesn't keep around a bunch of herbs or a mortar and pestle?

Kitchen witchery is also very practical and usually inexpensive, because it uses things that most of us have around the house anyway. Want to do a prosperity spell? Use a few herbs and bake some magickal bread. Need to work some love magick? Whip up a batch of chocolate cupcakes and put some frosting roses on top. Healing magick is as simple as a cup of herbal tea.

There are many great books out there that tell you how to be a Kitchen Witch, but truly all you need is a few spell basics and a little imagination.

So what are you waiting for? Go and cook up something magickal!

Required Reading: "Witch in the Kitchen"

If you are looking for a book that has great recipes for Pagans along with hints on kitchen witchery, you can't do any better than Cait Johnson's *Witch in the Kitchen: Magical Cooking for All Seasons*.

In Part 1, she tells you how to make your kitchen a sacred space, gives suggestions on making a kitchen altar, and even throws in some instructions for making a sexy Kitchen Witch apron! The rest of the book combines wonderful kitchen spells and rituals with tasty recipes for every season (like Demeter's Soothing Oat-Bread Soup and Aphrodite's Love Cakes—try that one out, and let me know if it works!)

Dear Magic the Cat,

How do cats always know when you're going to do something interesting in the kitchen? It seems as though as soon as I think about going into the kitchen, my cat is already there. It is a little spooky. Also, it sometimes makes it hard to do my magickal work. Is there something I can do to get a moment in the kitchen without feline supervision?

Confused Kitchen Witch

Dear Confused,

Sorry, no. All cats are born with two things: the psychic ability to know when something interesting is going on in their favorite room in the house and the supernatural speed to get there before the good stuff starts. It is just in our nature. My suggestion is to simply learn to make the best of it. After all, my Witch loves it when I am underfoot while she is brewing up something magickal—she says that in our house, cat fur is the secret ingredient in every magickal potion.

Familiarly,
Magic the Cat

Witch 101:
"Kisses"

Kisses have traditionally been used in ritual by covens based on the more organized forms of Wicca, those that tend to follow the high priest/high priestess levels of initiation group practice. In his book *Wicca for Life*, Raymond Buckland calls this sort of kiss a "salute" and explains that it is done to acknowledge the sacredness of the body (as representing the goddess and god within us).

In my group, we don't do anything more than the usual kiss on the cheek—or, if we're really being formal, both cheeks. And of course, if you are lucky enough to have a partner who is also a Witch, you can practice the Great Rite, starting with lots and lots of magickal kisses. (Sigh.) Thankfully, for the rest of us, there are always the chocolate kind ...

laughter

Lammas

love

lapis lazuli

LAUGHTER

One of the things that appeals to me most about being a Pagan is our attitude toward laughter. Unlike some of the gloomier religions out there, Witches do not consider laughter to be an optional extra (at best) or an insult to god (at worst).

This is not to say that people who follow other spiritual paths don't do their share of laughing, but it doesn't usually take place during the actual service. Witches, on the other hand, are actually *supposed* to have a sense of humor about such things. In fact, the Charge of the Goddess bids us to celebrate our rituals "with reverence and mirth."

I think that this is a good thing, especially since in my experience it is a rare ritual that goes off without a hitch: candles refusing to light or stay lit, people forgetting the words to the chant, realizing halfway through that no one brought the bread for the cakes...

If these things are taken seriously, it can really affect the magickal energy in the circle and lessen the effectiveness of whatever witchy work you are trying to achieve. On the other hand, if everyone just laughs and carries on, that positive vibe helps to boost the energy even further. (Not to mention that it is just more fun.)

And while there are some Pagans out there, for sure, who are all about the gloom and doom, for the most part, the witchy people I know don't take themselves that seriously. They can laugh at themselves and at each other (and at the mundanes we share our lives with, of course—but don't tell them that).

This is not to say that we don't take our religion seriously; we do. That's the reverence part of "reverence and mirth," and it is just as important to our spiritual practice as being able to laugh. But we need the balance between the two to keep us in balance—with ourselves, with each other, and with the often confusing and troubling universe we live in.

So treat the gods and each other with reverence when it seems right to do so, but don't forget to laugh sometimes too—laughter can be as healing as a cup of herbal tea or a big piece of chocolate (and laughter has no calories).

Did you hear the one about the Witch, the Druid, and the Satanist?

Ask Onyx:
"She Who Laughs Last"

Dear Onyx,

Do you know any good jokes about Witches?

Humorous in Houston

Dear Humorous,

Well, you know how Witches always seem to be running late? (I've even heard it called PST—Pagan Standard Time!) Well...

Q: How do you know when it is midnight?

A: The nine o'clock ritual just started.

(Snicker.)

Bright blessings,
Onyx

Lammas

Lammas is the first of three Pagan harvest festivals, the other two being Mabon (in September) and Samhain (in October). It takes place on August 1 and is also sometimes known as Lughnasadh, after the Celtic god Lugh (pronounced Lew-NAH-sah and Lew, respectively, in case you were wondering).

Lugh is a god of light, and Lammas/Lughnasadh is a celebration of light, food, and life.

Harvest festivals are a particularly important part of Pagan lore, and not just because they are a great excuse to eat, drink, and be merry (although that certainly doesn't hurt). They remind us of the importance of the land to our health and well-being.

Our Pagan roots go back to the days when people lived off the land and grew most of the food that they ate. There was no Piggly Wiggly down the street where you could go to grab a gallon of milk and a loaf of bread. You grazed your cow on the hay in your fields and milked her yourself, and you grew the wheat and oats for your bread. If the hay, wheat, and oats failed—in all likelihood, so did you.

So Pagans prayed to the gods for good harvests to sustain them and their families throughout the year and held big festivals to celebrate and thank the gods when the harvest was bountiful. The fact that there are three separate harvest holidays ought to give some indication of the importance of such things in Ye Olde Pagan Life.

So why do we still celebrate harvest festivals like Lammas now that we get most of our food from grocery stores, and much of that is grown many hundreds of miles away from where we live? Are they really still relevant to our lives as modern Pagans?

You bet your bippy they are. Not only do they serve as a connection to the Witches who came before us and in whose path we follow, but they also remind us to be more mindful of where our food comes from and what it goes through to get to us.

We take this opportunity to express our gratitude to those who labor to grow the food we pick up so effortlessly at the store and to remember that it wasn't always this easy. And those of us who do grow some of our own food happily share it with those who don't. In some versions of the Wheel of the Year, Lammas is the time when the god sacrifices himself so that life might continue. So take a moment to send appreciation to all those who sacrifice so that we might eat.

We may not be as obviously dependent on the land as our Pagan ancestors, but Lammas is a good time to be mindful of our continuing debt to our mother the earth and to say thank you out loud. We eat, drink, and are merry, but we also say a prayer for the health of the earth, because it is still true that if the land fails, so do we all.

LOVE

Love is a very important element in Witchcraft. So important, in fact, that we often say "love is the law." And when we practice together in circle, we do so in "perfect love and perfect trust." In theory, Witches love the goddess, the god (in whichever form you worship her/him), each other, the rest of the world, and themselves. Piece of cake, right?

Okay, okay—I hear you. How, you say, can love be a law? (I mean, seriously—who enforces that one? "Open up, it's the Pagan police—you're not being loving enough!") What the heck is perfect love? And who can realistically be expected to love everyone, all the time, no matter how annoying they might be?

First of all, you're right, of course. There is no actual law, there is no such thing as perfect love, and no one can possibly love everyone all the time (not even Gandhi—and most of us are no Gandhi).

So why do Witches put so much emphasis on love if all this is unattainable by any of us imperfect, living-in-the-real-world folks? In part, because it is something to aim for—a major goal and tough to achieve—but still something that we try to make a part of our witchy practice. Also, our gods are all about love. In the Charge of the Goddess, it says, "Her law is love unto all beings" and "Keep pure your highest ideal and ever strive towards it." (It also says "all acts of love and pleasure are her rituals," but that's a different topic...)

So we, as Witches, try the best we can to live up to the ideal of love for all, and do what we can to pass on the love that our goddess gives so freely to us.

This is why our spiritual beliefs tell us to be open and nonjudgmental, and to accept all those around us as being perfect just the way they are (some of them may be perfectly annoying...but they're still perfect). And this is why it is important that we learn to love ourselves just as we are.

This may be the hardest task the goddess sets before us, but it is, nonetheless, one of the most important objectives for Witches: to learn to love ourselves and those around us as fully and as freely as possible.

Quintessential Quotes:
"Lotsa Love"

The law of the Goddess is love: passionate sexual love, the warm affection of friends, the fierce protective love of mother for child, the deep comradeship of the coven. There is nothing amorphous or superficial about love in Goddess religion; it is always specific, directed toward real individuals, not vague concepts of humanity. Love includes animals, plants, the earth itself—all beings, not just human beings. It includes ourselves and all our fallible human qualities.
—Starhawk, *The Spiral Dance*

So I wish you love in all of its many glorious permutations: romantic love, spiritual love, the love between child and parent, brother and sister, between friends, and between us and the animals who share their lives with us. Most of all, I wish you the love of a bunch of wacky Witches, whether they are your group or just a few folks who come together for the occasional celebration, because it has been my experience that when it comes to Pagans, love really *is* the law and a major part of the shining glory that is Witchcraft.

Lapis Lazuli

Lapis lazuli (lah-zoo-lee) is another one of those great all-around, good for everything gemstones. Like amethyst, it tends to be expensive; but if you are a Witch, it is a stone well worth investing in.

Lapis is a blue stone, ranging in color from a vivid royal blue with flecks of gold (well, pyrite, actually, but it looks like gold) to a darker navy blue with a little bit of white. The first type is more valuable and therefore more expensive, but they should both work equally well in magick. Throughout history, lapis has been associated with kings and queens, and it is sacred to both Isis and Venus.

Lapis is used for healing (as are most blue stones), joy, love, fidelity (although from what I remember of my history lessons, that may not have worked so well for all those kings and queens), beauty, prosperity, protection, courage, and to increase psychic ability. I did tell you it was good for just about everything!

I consider lapis lazuli to be especially good for healing work (try pairing it with hematite for extra oomph) or any magick involving the spirit. It can be worn to strengthen the spiritual bonds between lovers or to aid in meditation or relieve depression. It is said to open the mind to intuition, so try using it when scrying or reading tarot cards.

If you have a goddess altar, you may want to put out a piece of lapis as an offering. You could also place a piece somewhere in your child's room, since it is supposed to be particularly protective for children. Lapis makes especially lovely jewelry, so consider making or buying a lapis necklace and pairing it with a favorite pentacle.

However you use it, lapis lazuli is a truly powerful and spiritual stone and one that is sure to serve you well in all your magickal endeavors.

Charmed, I'm Sure:
"Lapis Lazuli Lift"

If you are feeling blue and want to give yourself a boost both physically and mentally, try making this simple charm:

In a blue cloth or bag, place a piece of lapis lazuli and some lavender. Take a piece of paper and draw a smiley face on it while visualizing yourself feeling happy and healthy. Put the paper in the bag with the lapis (if you are using a cloth, tie a piece of string or yarn around it to hold it closed). Then hold the bag in your hands and spend a few minutes filling it with positive energy.

Say: "Lavender lovely and lapis blue, health and harmony through and through." Put it on your altar or under your pillow, but be sure to take it out and hold it for a few minutes every day. You should be feeling better in no time!

Magic's Herbal Helpers:
"*Lavender Lightness*"

Lavender is a powerful healing and purifying plant, and it is also used for love and peace magick (although not necessarily at the same time!). Lavender has the benefit of being easy to find and simple to use, so with very little effort it can be incorporated into magickal baths, sachets, charms, and incenses.

Traditionally, Witches throw lavender into the bonfire at Midsummer as a sacrifice to the Old Gods. It can be rubbed on love letters or grown by the front door if you want to attract love to your house. Medicinally, lavender is used to calm and bring sleep, and it is good for those purposes in magickal work as well. Place some lavender in a sachet and tuck it under your pillow to help you fall sleep. Sweet dreams!

Elemental Essentials:
"Lunar Eclipse"

Lunar eclipses happen a couple of times a year, and they are always powerful magickal events. According to Dorothy Morrison, a lunar eclipse "provides a time when the energies of the Moon and Sun connect, and this marriage of sorts brings a balance, an equalization of the male and female polarities if you will, that puts everything back into perspective."[8]

A lunar eclipse can be so powerful, it is a good time to do magick to achieve your most important and difficult-to-attain goals. You can also use the special energy of the eclipse to do magick for balance or protection. Just be sure to focus carefully and don't try anything too lunatic, since magick done on this night can last for a very long time.

Wit from the World Wide Web:
"Let There Be Light"

Q: How many Gardnerians does it take to change a light bulb?

A: "Sorry, that's a Third Degree mystery."

Q: How many Alexandrians does it take to change a light bulb?

A: "Let's go see how the Gardnerians do it!"

---

8   Morrison, *Everyday Moon Magic*, 45.

Q: How many British Traditional Witches does it take to change a light bulb?

A: Thirteen: one to change the bulb and twelve to mourn the old bulb's passing.

Q: How many Druids does it take to change a light bulb?

A: Druids don't screw in light bulbs—they screw in stone circles!

Q: How many fam-trad Witches does it take to change a light bulb?

A: "Candlelight was good enough for our ancestors; it's good enough for us!"

Q: How many Solitary Witches does it take to change a light bulb?

A: Only one—but they have to read a lot of books on how to do it first.

Q: How many Wiccans does it take to change a light bulb?

A: Four: one for each direction.

Q: How many ceremonial magicians does it take to change a light bulb?

A: One: he holds up the light bulb and the world revolves around him.

Q: How many Witches does it take to change a light bulb?

A: "What do you want it changed into?"

Q: How many Pagans does it take to change a light bulb?

A: Six: one to change the bulb and five to sit around complaining about how light bulbs never burned out before the Christians came along.

mundanes

magick

motherhood

Mabon

Midsummer

moon

MUNDANES

Witches often use the word *mundane* to mean any person who is not a Pagan. That is to say, "them" as opposed to "us." It is not meant as an insult (at least not most of the time) but rather as an explanatory label, as in the case of "Oh, yes, my husband Joe is a mundane, but he's pretty flexible about me going to rituals." (Apparently the "official" word is *cowan*, but I've never heard anyone use it. In fact, since *Harry Potter* came out, you're much more likely to hear the term *muggle*.)

But what does the word mean, and why do we use that word and not something else?

Interestingly, if you look up mundane in the dictionary (as I knew you were all going to do if I didn't do it for you), you will find the following definition: "of, relating to or characteristic of the world or characterized by the practical, transitory and ordinary—commonplace."

You can easily see why we apply this label to them and not to us, since Witches tend to be anything but ordinary and commonplace. But it is also an indication that there are a lot more of them than there are of us; the world is made up of mundanes, not (alas) Pagans. In fact, the word comes from the Latin for "world."

The word also implies the notion that while mundanes are "of the world," we Pagans tend to be more involved in the otherworldly, or at least more aware of and in touch with those things that are not so much practical, transitory, and ordinary.

So in a way, by defining those who are not us, we are defining ourselves. We are all at least in part mundane—we are connected to the everyday world by our jobs, our relationships with non-Pagan others, and by the ordinary necessities of survival. But we are also Witches and live in a world that the mundanes who surround us cannot even imagine.

Helpful Hints:
"Married to a Mundane"

Many Witches are married to or involved with non-Witches. This can be tough when we want to share a piece of our magickal lives with them, but they are not comfortable attending rituals. (Can you believe it? Some of those lovely folks actually think we're kind of...uh, weird.) An easy compromise is to have the ritual first, with Witches only, and then include all the mundanes in the feasting afterwards. This way everyone is happy.

MAGICK

We talk a lot about magick, but what is it?

There are probably as many definitions of magick as there are Witches. Some say that it is will made manifest. Others say that it is the use of powers available to all but acknowledged by few. Or that it is intent focused strongly enough to effect change in the universe.

All of these are true. But I like the definition that Eileen Holland uses in her (very good) book *The Wicca Handbook*—she says simply that magick is "the manipulation of energy to achieve a desired result."[9]

Nothing spooky or supernatural, but rather a natural byproduct of the human wish to create a better world for oneself. Holland also says that "magic is about empowerment." About making ourselves stronger, wiser, and (with any luck) better people. To me, this pretty well sums it up.

---

9 Holland, *The Wicca Handbook*, 29.

So how do we go about making improvements in our world and in ourselves using magick? Traditionally, there are four steps, which are as follows:

To Will—This is essentially the desire to create positive change and the belief that such change is possible. Without both the desire and the belief, Witchcraft can't be done.

To Know—You need to have knowledge of what you are trying to achieve (a clear idea of what you are intending to do) and knowledge of how to do it (the actual steps of the spell).

To Do—Actually doing the spell. This requires energy from you, and the more energy you put into a spell and the more focused that energy is, the more powerful your magickal working will be.

To Be Silent—Once you have done the work, shut up and get on with your life. Seriously. It is tempting to talk about the magick once you have completed the spell, but this can easily weaken the work you put so much time and energy into doing. If you want to confer with your fellow Witches about how you are going to cast a spell, do it before, not after. Once the magick is sent out into the universe, just let it be what it is going to be.

All four of these components are necessary to successfully work magick. The good news is that they are free, simple, and readily available to any Witch who wants to use them. All you really need is a little patience and the will to make it so.

The concept of motherhood is key to Pagan beliefs, including both Mother Earth and the mother personification of the goddess's triple form of maiden, mother, and crone.

But *being* a Witch and a mother can be a little bit more complicated.

The five women in my circle who are parents have covered the entire gamut of the Witch-as-mother experience: pregnant (no wine in the chalice for cakes and ale), breastfeeding an infant (ditto, plus the baby gets passed around the circle during ritual so Mom actually gets to take part), small toddlers (by all means bring him/her to the sabbat, but *please* not to the full moon rite while we're trying to concentrate), teenager, and young adult (your kid wants to know more about Witchcraft? You bet you can bring him/her!). It has been interesting, to say the least.

If you are a Solitary mother Witch, things may be simpler (mostly a matter of hiding the dangerous herbs and trying to find an hour *somewhere* to be by yourself to work magick), but you still have to deal with the tricky issues of which holidays to celebrate with your child and worrying about what might or might not be said at school.

If you are a group mother Witch, you have the added complication of trying to keep the other folks in your witchy gang happy as well. Not everyone wants to have children in circle—some Pagans find it disruptive, and others just don't think it is appropriate to expose young kids to the sometimes intense energy generated by doing active magick.

Each group has to make these decisions for themselves, taking into account the needs and wants of everyone involved. Usually this necessitates a certain amount of compromise. Sometimes it involves finding a different group if the one you are in has child-unfriendly boundaries that you don't feel you can live with.

As far as having children in circle goes, my experience is that yes, it can be disruptive, and no, the energy doesn't seem to do them any harm.

On the other hand, being a mother is part of the natural cycle of things, and isn't that what being a Pagan is all about? And how can you pass on a religion if the next generation is never allowed to take part in it?

However you handle being both a Witch and a mother, if you share with your child the love of nature and your joy in your spiritual life, I'm sure that all the other dilemmas will eventually be resolved in a way that works out for all those concerned. After all, the goddess is a mother too, so I am certain that she has a soft spot in her heart for witchy moms.

Ask Onyx:
"Mother, May I?"

Dear Onyx,

My mother doesn't know I am a Witch, but every time I burn sage in my room, she thinks I'm smoking pot. What should I do?

Smelly in Saratoga

Dear Smelly,

I'm pretty sure that your mother would rather have you practicing a nature-based religion than doing drugs. Have you considered just talking to her about what you believe? Maybe buy her a simple book explaining Witchcraft? If you're sure that won't work, I'd switch to lavender incense. It will work just as well and is less likely to set off the maternal smoke alarm.

Bright blessings,
Onyx

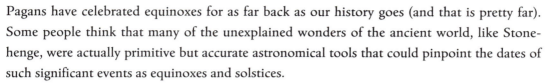

Pagans have celebrated equinoxes for as far back as our history goes (and that is pretty far). Some people think that many of the unexplained wonders of the ancient world, like Stonehenge, were actually primitive but accurate astronomical tools that could pinpoint the dates of such significant events as equinoxes and solstices.

And why would they want to do that? So they could celebrate, of course!

There are two equinoxes every year—Ostara, the Spring Equinox, which falls on or around March 21, (the actual date can vary from the 20th to the 22nd, so check your calendar or almanac) and Mabon, or the Autumn Equinox, which occurs on or around September 21.

Equinoxes can be used for magickal work (and often are), but mostly they are times for celebration and—my favorite—feasting!

Mabon celebrates the harvest, both actual and spiritual, of all those things that you have nurtured and grown throughout the year. As with its counterpart the Spring Equinox, the light and dark are again in perfect balance—and hopefully we are too! If not, this is a good time to start thinking about the things that will help us get there.

At Mabon, the god sleeps in the womb of his mother, the goddess, as he waits to be reborn at Yule. We celebrate because although the god sacrificed himself at Lammas, we know that he will come around again with the turning of the Wheel of the Year.

This is a great time to get together with your Pagan family and to include any members of your non-Pagan family who are open-minded and want to join in with the fun. So break out the mead, have everyone bring a dish to share (preferably one that is appropriate to the season you are celebrating, like harvest veggies and cider at Mabon), and add another link to the chain that connects us on down through the years to all the Pagans that preceded us and all those who will follow.

MIDSUMMER

Midsummer is the sabbat that falls on the Summer Solstice (on or around June 21) and is also known as Litha. It is the longest day of the year, with the most light and the least dark, and the earth is at her most fertile. The land is full of energy and life; the goddess as mother is pregnant, and her consort the god is at the height of his powers. It is time to party and rejoice! (Like we really need an excuse for that.)

Midsummer is a time to celebrate family and love. It is a traditional day for handfasting rites (Pagan wedding ceremonies), and some Witches do divination now to help them find their true loves. If you've already found yours, be sure to celebrate that, too!

The Summer Solstice is also said to be the optimal day on which to harvest your magickal and medicinal herbs for use in the year ahead (which works really well if your growing season is such that these plants are actually ready to be harvested, of course—where I live, we just take a ritual clipping of each plant and call it good).

In the Pagan mythos, Midsummer marks the end of the waxing part of the year, ruled by the Oak King, and starts the waning half of the year, ruled by the Holly King. (At Midsummer's counterpart, the Winter Solstice, or Yule, this is reversed, and the Oak King battles the Holly King to regain his throne.)

Witches celebrate Midsummer with strawberries and mead and feasts of summer foods. It is traditional to throw lavender into the bonfire as a sacrifice to the Old Gods (if at all possible, you *have* to have a bonfire). Some years my group throws in scraps of paper with the crap we want out of our lives written on them—willing sacrifices that we hope will leave more room for the positive potential of the energetic summer season.

Whether you celebrate alone or with others, be sure to take advantage of the powerful energy from earth and sun that is so abundant at this time of year, and take a moment to give thanks for all the blessings you are harvesting in your own life.

Historically, Witches have always been very connected to the moon. Many of the Witch goddesses are also moon goddesses, such as Hecate and Diana. We do our magick at full moons and new moons. Some folks even use the moon to decide when to plant. But what is it about the moon that makes it so magickal?

I don't know. (What, you thought I had the answers to everything? Silly you.) But I do have a few theories.

For one thing, the moon has a physical effect on all human beings and on the world around us. Even ancient man knew about the connection between the moon and the tides, and could see that people often felt and acted differently under the influence of the full moon. For another, there is the cycle of waxing and waning, which is symbolic of the greater cycle of birth, growth, death, and rebirth. Either way, Witches have worshipped with and under the moon since the beginning of time.

It is important to remember that the full moon, while an important time for magick, isn't the only time to do spellwork. All of the phases of the moon have their uses; you just need to figure out which phases are best for the magickal work you want to do.

The lunar cycle is generally broken up into waxing and waning times, with the full moon and the dark moon at the cusps. The waning period, which starts the day after the full moon and runs until the dark moon, is used for magick concerning decrease, as opposed to the waxing period (dark moon until full), which is used for increase.

What does this mean for witchy workings? Well, if you want to do magick for prosperity, for example, you could do a spell during the waning moon to decrease your debt and one during the waxing moon to increase your income. Simple!

As with all other witchy issues, there is a fair amount of disagreement about things like what to use the dark moon for, or whether there are times when you should not do magick at all. My suggestion is to listen to your heart (and to the moon herself), and just do what feels right to you at the time. After all, you're a Witch, a child of the moon, and magick is in your blood. Feel it change along with the tides, and just go with the flow!

Required Reading:
"Books for Lunatics"

For those who want to learn more about moon-related magick, here are two great books:

Everyday Moon Magic: Spells & Rituals for Abundant Living by Dorothy Morrison (Llewellyn, 2003)

Rituals of the Dark Moon: 13 Lunar Rites for a Magical Path by Gail Wood (Llewellyn, 2001). This book focuses on the power of the dark moon and offers a very different slant on lunar magick; I recommend it highly.

Food of the Gods:
"Merry Mead"

Mead is a very witchy kind of wine made from honey. It is one of the oldest alcoholic drinks and one of the easiest to make, although you have to have patience—the process takes about a year. Mead can be flavored with berries for an even more fanciful drink. Be sure to share it with the faeries, who are said to be particularly partial to honey wines.

Magic the Cat's Simple Spells:
"Dark Moon Magick"

The dark moon (when the moon is not visible) is a great time to do self-exploration magick. If you want to take a closer look at the mystery that is you, try this simple spell during the dark moon period:

Take a large clear quartz crystal or a bowl of water outside to someplace quiet. (If you have to be inside, turn out all the lights to simulate the darkness of the moonless night.) Light a black candle and place it in front of you, with the crystal or bowl of water in between you and the candle so the light shines on it.

Concentrate on your desire to see inside yourself, and say the following: "Dark moon on a quiet night, help me see my inner light." Then look into your crystal or water to see what the moon has to tell you.

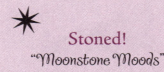

Stoned!
"Moonstone Moods"

Moonstone is a gemstone that is, as its name would suggest, closely associated with the moon. As such, it is also a sacred goddess stone and is considered to have many of the powers ascribed to the moon itself. It is a mottled milky-white gem with a subtle gleam. Rainbow moonstone even has shimmers of light color and can be astonishingly beautiful. It is sometimes worn by Witches (especially high priestesses) during full moon rituals.

Moonstone is often used with psychic work, to boost intuition, and to aid in divination. Some psychics keep a moonstone with their cards or runes. If you can find a large moonstone, it can even be used as a "crystal" ball. The stone is also used for love, protection, and sleep magick. I have even read that it is good for diet magick…but be careful that you don't end up waning, only to wax full again!

nature

never

naked

names

NATURE

Along with our belief in the goddess, probably the other single most important element of the witchy way that sets us apart from other religions is our bond with nature. Paganism is a nature-based religion, and much of the practice of Witchcraft is tied to various aspects of nature, including moon cycles, seasonal changes, and the many gifts that come to us from the natural world.

Paganism comes in many different forms—Native American, Druid, Wicca, and more—and some folks follow old paths handed down through the ages, while others create new paths to suit a modern Witch's changing needs. What brings us together is a common belief in the importance of our connection to nature and our insistence that the world around us be treated with care and respect.

If you look at the standard Judeo-Christian religions that most of us were raised in, you will see that man (as in human beings, not just you guys) is seen to be superior to nature—not only set apart from it, but set *above* it. The natural world is seen as something that god gave to humanity to use as we please. This attitude probably goes a long way toward explaining why the world we live in is now such a crappy mess.

Witches, on the other hand, believe that we are a *part* of nature—and not necessarily a big, important part, either. Just a piece of a greater whole, much of which is more powerful than we are. (Seriously—have you ever tried to argue with a tornado, or even a large wave? We are little, puny creatures.)

As Witches, we not only use much of nature in our rituals (herbs, gemstones, feathers, etc.) and follow the Wheel of the Year through the changing seasons, but we also celebrate our place in the natural world with gratitude and appreciation.

If you are a Witch, odds are that you tend a garden, compost, recycle, drive a car that doesn't
guzzle gas, and do as many other things as possible to preserve what is left of our beautiful
Mother Earth. Even if you live in a city, you can join the Arbor Foundation and plant a tree. (Or
twelve. Really, your mother would want you to.)

This is what it means to be part of a nature-based religion: that as we live our day-to-day lives,
we tend and nurture the mother who tends and nurtures us. Have you planted a tree lately?

Quintessential Quotes:
"Natural Magick"

*Natural magick is intended to show you ways that various
gifts from the Earth combined with your natural talents dance
together. Herbs, crystals, astrology, sacred tools, intuition,
visualization, and divination—together these create natural
magick. The more intricate the music, the more divine the
dance, the more wonderful the magick performed.*
— Sally Dubats, *Natural Magick*

Ask Magic the Cat:
"It's Only Natural"

Dear Magic the Cat,

My Witch says she is all about nature, but when I bring her little gifts like dead mice, birds, or chipmunks, she always screams and throws them out of the house. Aren't they part of nature too?

Perplexed in Paramus

Dear Perplexed,

Well, I can see why this is confusing, especially since Witches are always bringing in objects from nature to put on their altars. I'm not really sure why a feather is fine but the whole bird is a problem, but this is one of those areas where you just have to do what makes them happy. It's not their fault they're so mixed up; they're only humans, after all. Just humor her, and keep your bits of nature outside—not only will your Witch be happier, but she'll think you haven't eaten and feed you again.

Familiarly,
Magic the Cat

One of the best parts of being a Witch is that there are hardly any rules. You gotta love that. Really, we only have one: *An it harm none, do as ye will.* So pretty much as long as what you do doesn't hurt anyone (including yourself), it's cool.

But there are a few things that are considered to be serious no-noes in the witchy world. They may not get you sent to hell (since Witches don't actually believe in hell, the devil, or, for that matter, sin), but they could get you severely scolded by your witchy friends. (Or, worse yet, get your butt kicked by the karma police.)

So as you make your way through your day, keep in mind that you should NEVER, EVER:

- Cast a spell that will hurt anyone (see Rule #1, above).

- Cast a spell that interferes with another person's free will (even if you are sure it will help them).

- "Out" someone as a Witch without asking them first—if you don't know whether or not someone is out of the broom closet, do not mention their witchiness to anyone.

- Tell outsiders what goes on in your group rituals (unless it is okay with all members).

- Break circle during a ritual (this can scatter or burst the gathered energy with unpleasant effects). If it is necessary to leave mid-ritual, you should be "cut" out of circle.

- Pick up someone else's witchy tools (athame, tarot cards, drums, etc.) without asking first. These tools become attuned to their user's energy with repeated use, and some Witches don't like to have their own energy diluted or contaminated by someone else's.

- Cast a spell to make someone else love you. Not only does this interfere with free will, but it is likely to come back and bite you on the butt eventually. Seriously—I know it can be tempting, but just don't do it. (You can cast a spell to make yourself open to love instead, which will only affect you, so it is okay.)

- Force someone to take part in a ritual or any other aspect of witchy life if they don't want to. If your friends, relatives, or co-workers are meant to be Pagans, they'll come to you when the time is right and they are ready. We want others to respect our spiritual beliefs—that means we have to do the same. (This is especially true for significant others. We all want to share our lives with someone who believes as we do, but sometimes we just have to settle for tolerance instead of agreement.)

- Talk to outsiders about a confidence shared with you in circle. We have a saying: "What's said in circle stays in circle." (Yeah, I know, those Vegas people stole it from us.) People need to know that if they bare their souls while passing the speaking stick—or at any other point during ritual—that whatever they talk about will stay in the safe space of circle and not show up as gossip in the outside world.

There are probably a few more that I am forgetting, but these are the biggies. Avoid these "nevers" and do harm to none, and you can practice your craft with a clear conscience and a happy heart.

There is a simple word that can strike fear into the heart of the bravest Witch: skyclad.

Arrggghhhh! (See, told you.)

Skyclad is the word we use to mean, well, nude. As in, "This month's full moon ritual will be done skyclad."

Starkers, as the Brits say. In your birthday suit. Sans clothing. In your altogether. In short, buck-naked. Or as my dad used to say, "stark, nuked nade."

Either way, it means you are out there under the moon with the breeze blowing through your, er…everything.

Some Witches are very comfortable practicing skyclad. Others wouldn't do it on a bet. Still others save such dedication for their solitary rituals and prefer to wear garb when gathering with their fellow Witches.

All of the above is fine. There is no rule that says you have to perform Witchcraft naked (thank the goddess), although there are some traditions where that is the norm. And although in the Charge of the Goddess it says "ye shall be naked in your rites," this doesn't mean that you have to stand outside at midwinter freezing your whatsits off.

As with most things witchy, you should use your own judgment and do what feels right to you. If you're comfortable being naked, by all means do your rituals skyclad. If you're not, you would probably find your nakedness so distracting that you wouldn't be able to concentrate on your magick anyway, so there's not much point to it.

The important thing to remember is that in the case of group rituals, you should discuss such things ahead of time and make sure that everyone agrees. There isn't much that is more disconcerting than showing up at a ritual to find out that you are expected to disrobe when you weren't planning on it.

Arrggghhhh!

Magic the Cat's Simple Spells:
"Naked in Your Sight"

If you want to do some "naked" magick but are too uncomfortable to stand around in your living room in your altogether, try doing this simple spell while in the bath or shower (where, presumably, you'll be naked anyway):

Close your eyes and visualize your naked body in a waterfall or pond. See the water as the physical manifestation of the energy of the universe, and take in as much of that energy as you can hold. Then say, "As I was born, I am at this hour, fill my body with your power."

NAMES

Names are important. Everybody knows this. Pregnant women spend hours poring over books of names to find the perfect moniker for their little Witch-to-be. Movie stars change their names to sound more, well, movie star-like. Some people even name their cars. (Merrie Grace, I miss you!)

Witches and other magickal workers have always known that names have power. In Egyptian mythology, the Witch goddess Isis is said to have used her magick to discover the secret name of the sun god Ra and thus gain power over him. In some cultures, children are given "use names" until they are old enough to find their real name for themselves, or their names are kept secret so that evil spirits can't cause harm.

Witches have traditionally taken on a "Witch name." In the good-old, bad-old days, that may have been done in part as a way to keep one's identity a secret from non-Witches. These days, a Witch name may be taken as part of a Witch's formal dedication or simply adopted along the way. Mine came to me as a gift from one of the members of the original group I practiced with: we were talking one evening about Witch names, and I was bemoaning the fact that I had never found one that seemed right to me, when one of the guys turned to me and said, "Of course you have a Witch name—it's Onyx." And so it was.

Ann Moura, in her book *Green Witchcraft: Folk Magic, Fairy Lore & Herb Craft*, points out that there are actually two different kinds of Witch names. One, which she calls the Craft name, is chosen by the Witch and used in public. My name Onyx is one of these—it appears in my books where everyone can see it and is in no way intended to be secret.

The other type of Witch name, which Moura calls the "working" name, is a gift which is bestowed upon the Witch by the god and goddess. This name has more power and should be used only when speaking to the gods (as in "I, _____, beseech you") or when working with the magickal folks that you trust the most. Don't worry if this one doesn't come to you right away; I've been practicing for many years and just got my working name a few months ago. (No, I'm not going to tell you what it is!)

The important thing to keep in mind is that names do have power. So choose carefully when you pick a Witch name—make sure that it is one that means something to you and that it feels powerful and right. Witches can and do change their names over the course of their practice, as they themselves grow and change, but you are better off waiting for the right name to come to you—as I did—than picking just any old name in order to have one. For now, I'll just call you Bubba.

Ask Magic the Cat:
"Cat Names"

Dear Magic the Cat,

Someone told my Witch recently that all cats have secret names, and now she is walking around the house reciting names in order to try and figure out what mine is. She started out with silly things like "Fluffy" and "Snookums" (I ask you—are there actually any cats named Snookums? And if so, do they ever come out from under the couch?), and today I heard her mutter something that sounded like Rumplestiltskin. (What's a rumplestiltskin, and is it edible?) Should I just give in and tell her my name so she'll cut it the heck out? She's driving me to catnip.

Secretive Sammy in Seattle

Dear Secretive,

Of course you can't tell her your name, you ninny—it's a secret! If all cats went around telling our humans our secret names, then where would we be? But I can tell that this is becoming a problem, so here's what you do: tonight while she is sleeping, whisper a name in her ear. It doesn't matter what it is, as long as it sounds like a good secret cat name. Try "Ambrose" or "Jabez"—I got those from one of my Witch's books (*Catspells: A Collection of Enchantments for You and Your Feline Companion* by Claire Nahmad). When she wakes up, she'll be sure she figured it out and leave you alone. And your secret name will stay a secret, as it should.

Familiarly,
Magic the Cat

ordination

Ostara

oils

ORDINATION

I am a Wiccan high priestess. In addition, I am also an ordained minister. No, really. (Will you stop? I can hear you snickering from here.)

At first glance, these two roles might seem to be contradictory, but there is actually a point to being both, and I know a number of high priests or high priestesses who have taken the step of becoming formally ordained.

Why would anyone do this? It's simple. In my case, one of my group members asked me to. You see, she wanted to get married to her longtime fiancé. And she wanted me, as her high priestess, to do the ceremony. (In fact, they both wanted me—which was even more flattering because he was a non-Pagan.)

The catch, of course, is that while our religion gives me the right to marry people, the laws of our country mean that such a marriage would not be legal—*unless* (wait for it) I was a legally ordained minister. Aha! Now you see where I am going with this.

So how did I become an ordained minister? Did I go to school for years and pay wads of money for the privilege? Not exactly. In fact, I went online and did it for free. (Right, now you're interested.)

There are a number of sites that offer free ordination. I would strongly caution you against most of them. My research showed me that many such sites, while legal, were all about money or power or other things that I considered inconsistent with the title that they offered. The one I ended up using is called Universal Ministries, and I picked them because they seem to honestly believe that all people have the right to become ordained ministers as long as they take the title and accompanying duties seriously.

And this is a point that I think you should consider before taking this step. I believe that Pagans should be able to have legal ceremonies just as non-Pagans do, so it is important for some members of our community to take on this role. I also believe, however, that such a step should not be taken lightly or just for fun.

"Ordained minister" is a title that bears with it certain responsibilities, just as being a high priest or high priestess does, and you should be sure that you are willing to take them on before you decide to go that extra mile. After all, in theory at least, you are binding two people together for life. And as we in the witchy world know, binding is very powerful magick indeed.

Because I got ordained, my circle-sister Robin was able to realize her desire to be married by her high priestess using some witchy customs while still having a ceremony that satisfied her non-Pagan hubby-to-be and both sets of non-Pagan parents. And she and her husband now have two beautiful children, who will be raised to know the best of both parents' worlds and—who knows—may someday choose to follow in their mother's witchy footsteps.

OSTARA

Ostara is the name of the holiday most Witches observe on the day of the Spring Equinox, which falls on or around March 21. Like its counterpart the Fall Equinox (Mabon), Ostara is notable for its unusual natural equilibrium—only on these two days of the year are the day and the night equal. Since the light and the dark are in perfect balance, this is a wonderful time for Witches to do magick that will help them to find balance in their own lives. (Who doesn't need help with that?)

Ostara is also symbolic of the change in the goddess from winter's crone to spring's maiden. The holiday calls to the youthful spirit within us all, no matter what our age, and celebrates the land's slow rebirth after the deathlike sleep of winter.

Witches observe the holiday with rituals and feasts, and decorate their altars with the traditional fertility symbols of rabbits, chicks, and eggs (no, not *actual* rabbits and chicks, although you are welcome to try it if you're feeling brave and don't mind cleaning up poop).

And if those symbols sound a bit familiar to those of you raised in one of the Christian religions, it is because many of the traditions of Easter were adopted from Ostara. Even the name

Easter was taken from a Pagan goddess: Eostre, a Saxon goddess of spring. Think about it: the symbols of Easter all represent fertility (those same eggs, chicks, and rabbits)—*much* more suitable for a Pagan holiday than a Christian one. Oh, the things they didn't tell you in Sunday school...

So adorn your altar with a few beautiful early spring flowers, draw some Pagan symbols on eggs before you dye them, and prepare a feast of traditional spring foods like asparagus and lamb. If you want, you can even plant a few seeds. Then, alone or with other Witches, plant the seeds for the changes you wish to occur in your life during the coming year.

Witch 101:
"Coloring Ostara Eggs"

Coloring traditional Ostara eggs is a fun activity that can be shared with your kids or with your group. All you need are some white eggs (hard-boil them first to avoid messy accidents), some crayons, various dyes, and an empty egg carton to put them in while they dry. Use the crayons to draw Pagan symbols or runes on the eggs (suns are good for this holiday and easy for kids to draw), then dye them in the colors of your choice. If you want to get back to your Pagan roots a bit more, you can use natural dyes made from such things as tea, grape juice, beets, or onion skins. And don't forget to have fun!

When you are putting together your witchy toolkit, don't forget to throw in a few oils. No, I'm not talking about canola or olive oil (although I'm sure that Kitchen Witches will find some uses for those). The oils I mean are special oils, typically ones that are blessed and consecrated for magickal use.

Usually the oils used by Witches for magickal purposes are derived from essential oils—the pure oil of a plant, unadulterated by chemicals or additives. These oils retain the essence of the plant (hence the name) and therefore the powers of the flower, herb, or tree from which they were taken.

While it is possible to use perfume oils for magickal work, these oils are produced artificially, so they are not likely to be as powerful as an essential oil (although most of them are much cheaper). My advice, for what it's worth, is that it is better to get a small amount of a true oil if it is expensive (such as rose or chamomile) and save it for special occasions than resort to the cheaper but less natural substitutes.

Some of the oils used for magickal work are single oils—for instance, the oil known as High John, or John the Conqueror, is often used to boost the power of a spell—while others are combinations of oils that are well-suited for a particular task (a purification oil might be made by combining grapefruit, lemongrass, and peppermint essential oils).

Witches often make their own combinations and store them in nifty bottles or flasks, but if you'd rather not mess about with such things (and oils can be messy), there are many good sources for pre-made magickal oils. (AzureGreen is one of my favorite sources for magickal oils, and you can find them both online and at your favorite Pagan store.)

Either way, these can be both fun and useful. And if you are feeling particularly imaginative, maybe you can come up with an interesting magickal body oil to share with someone you love…

Magic the Cat's Simple Spells:
"Magickal Healing Oil"

Here is a recipe for a simple healing oil my Witch makes:

Use a good base oil like sesame or jojoba (which doesn't turn rancid like most oils do). Olive oil will do if that's all you have. Add three drops each of calendula, lavender, lemon balm, and rosemary essential oils. If you can only find three of the four, that's fine. Gently swirl the oil in your bottle or vial nine times in a clockwise (deosil) direction while saying the following:

Earth, fire, water, air
Bless this oil that I prepare.

You can then use the oil by putting a few drops on a candle, in a bath, or on yourself. (Do not drink it. Seriously. It wouldn't hurt you, but it tastes like crap. Trust me on this.)

Elemental Essentials:
"Onyx"

Onyx is my favorite stone, and not just because it is my Witch name. Onyx is most often found as a black stone but also can be found in a natural tan, green, and blue. It is a very powerful protective gem, and it is also used for strength, balance, self-control, and defensive magick.

prosperity

pentacle

partners

psychic abilities

protection

perfect love
and perfect trust

P

PROSPERITY

Witches cast spells to achieve all sorts of goals—some of the most common are love, strength, protection, healing, and purification. But probably the most widely used spells are those for prosperity.

Prosperity means different things to different people. For some it means being able to pay the monthly bills without worry. For others it means the fulfillment of a specific goal (like an author selling a lot of her books, for instance, not that I would need to do magick for such a thing…). To some Witches it is about acquiring riches, for others it is more about lessening poverty.

In general, though, prosperity spells are aimed at removing the stress that not having enough money can cause, leaving us free to focus on other more important aspects of our lives. (It is hard to be spiritual when they are turning off the electricity, after all.)

As a Witch, I'm sure that it will come as no surprise to you when I say that I have seen prosperity spells work, sometimes amazingly well. Of course, like all spells, the gods sometimes grant your request in a form that you may not have anticipated. Full of surprises, those gods. So if you are going to do prosperity magick, try to do it in such a way that leaves the door open for positive things to happen in unexpected ways.

For instance, if you are an artist, you might do a spell to help you sell some of your work, only to end up being asked to teach instead. Keep an open mind, and wait and see what happens.

And while you're waiting, don't forget that the gods help those who help themselves. Doing magickal work is only the first step. If you need a new job, by all means cast a prosperity spell to help you find the right one—then get up off your butt and go looking. The spell may help direct your feet to the right path, but that only works if you are walking in the first place.

Magic the Cat's Simple Spells:
"Prosperity Possibilities"

Here is a simple prosperity spell. Notice the practical nature of the spell—it asks for specific things (pay off bills, lessen debt) and specifies that they come in positive ways. May it bring you what you need!

Turn the wheel of prosperity 'round
'Til gifts and money do abound
Pay off debt and manage bills
Compensate for living's ills
Abundance flows in positive ways
When money comes, money stays
All I wish for, all I need
I summon now with word and deed.

PENTACLE

The most common symbol used by witchy folks is a pentacle. A five-pointed star set within a circle, this symbol has come to represent Witchcraft in its many variations, and most Witches have at least one, whether it is worn on a chain around their necks or hung as a decoration on the wall above their altars.

Sadly, this beautiful symbol is mostly misunderstood by folks out in the mundane world. Too many years of Hollywood horror movies and Christian misrepresentation have left many people with the mistaken idea that the pentacle is a symbol of devil worship—when nothing could be further from the truth.

So what does the pentacle stand for, and what is the best way to explain it to the well-meaning but ignorant guy who asks you, "Hey, isn't that one of those satanic thingies?"

Here is what I tell people:

The pentacle is an ancient symbol that represents the beauty and balance of the natural world. The five-pointed star corresponds to the five elements: the basic four of earth, air, fire, and water, and the fifth element, which is spirit. The circle stands for the universe that surrounds them and for the unity of us all within that universe.

I know that it can get annoying to have to explain this over and over, but since the alternatives are to either never wear our pentacles in public or to allow such ignorance to flourish, it seems like a small price to pay for the right to wear our witchy symbol with pride.

In a perfect world, all Witches would live with or be married to other Witches who shared our spiritual beliefs and worshipped the Old Gods as we do. Right. Like that's ever going to happen!

The truth is, most of us aren't that lucky. (Some of us—we're not naming any names here—don't even have a partner at all.) But of the Witches that (a) want a partner and (b) actually have one, most end up with a significant other who is not a Pagan or even close. Some even end up with folks whose religious beliefs are diametrically opposed to their own. So how's a Witch to cope?

In my circle, three of the women are married, all to non-Pagans. The three husbands vary in the amount of interest/tolerance/bewilderment with which they view their wives' witchy lives, but they are all supportive and accepting in their own way. A couple of the guys usually come to our larger open holiday rituals, and all of them will at least show up for the feast afterwards, even if they are not comfortable taking part in the ritual itself. (Please—when's the last time you saw a guy pass up a free meal, much less a veritable feast?)

In turn, my witchy sisters have learned to tolerate their husbands' quirkier interests and appreciate them for the truly great (even if not Pagan) guys that they are.

We should all be so lucky.

In the end, I believe that it is more important to share the same basic values—family, friends, love, honesty, etc.—than it is to follow the same spiritual path. As long as you and your partner can agree to walk side by side through life, it doesn't matter if one of you is wearing a pentacle and the other is wearing a cross or a Star of David.

Relationships are always a matter of deciding which things you can compromise on and which things you can't. As long as your partner gives you the freedom to practice your craft and worship as you please, there is no reason why a relationship with a non-Pagan can't work out. (Remember that this has to go both ways, though—if your partner isn't interested in joining the witchy world, you need to respect that decision and not push your beliefs on him or her.)

Even if you are a Witch who is lucky enough to end up in a relationship with a fellow Pagan, you will undoubtedly have the occasional (ha!) moment of disagreement. Remember that perfect love and perfect trust applies to partners as much as to rituals, and I'm sure you'll do fine. And there's always make-up sex…

Psychic Abilities

Extrasensory perception, or ESP, is the ability to perceive things in ways that cannot be explained by normal means (such as sight, hearing, etc.). ESP is also sometimes referred to as the "sixth sense," or the "paranormal," and usually includes such talents as telepathy and clairvoyance, both of which are considered to be psychic abilities.

Psychic abilities of all kinds seem to crop up more often in Witches than in the population at large, although I couldn't give you any scientific studies to back that up. (I'm a Witch, not a physicist!) But I have a couple of theories as to why that is.

To begin with, the actual scientific studies (and there have been more dealing with ESP than you might think) seem to suggest that while all people may have a touch of extrasensory perception, it is more likely to show up strongly in people who believe in it and who are more intuitive and more relaxed. Well, duh—that's us! (At least some of us. I'm relaxed—aren't you?)

In addition, I think that those kinds of people—more relaxed, more intuitive, and more likely to believe the unlikely—are also more apt to be attracted to Witchcraft than the average person. That just makes sense. As does the fact that those with serious psychic abilities are likely to associate with people who will be comfortable with them, such as Witches, who are pretty much accepting of everyone.

So, if you are a Witch, does that mean you have extrasensory perception or some kind of psychic ability? Well, maybe. Do you read tarot cards and get answers that you have no other way of knowing? Do you predict that something will happen and then have it occur? Do you sometimes know who's calling when the phone rings? Do you dream about things that later come to pass? All of these things are indications of some kind of psychic ability, which, depending on who you are, can vary from barely noticeable "Gee, is this more than a coincidence?" to "Oh man, that's spooky!"

The more attention you pay to the "unusual" messages you get, the more likely you are to notice them when they happen. And there are some theories that suggest psychic ability can be honed and heightened through practice, meditation, trance work, and even yoga. Even keeping a pad and a pen by your bed to write down your dreams can help if you are interested in stretching your extrasensory muscles a bit.

If you are a Witch, odds are that you have at least a little bit of ESP. So why not put a pad and a pen by your bed tonight, and see what your dreams may bring? Who knows, maybe you'll dream about something magickal...

PROTECTION

Protection spells may be the most practical and useful magick that Witches do. And no, I'm not talking about conjuring up a condom before the Great Rite (although that's not a bad idea, come to think of it).

We live in a scary world. There are many dangers out there—some of them physical, some of them not. Negative energy and the ill wishes of others (even those not of a magickal bent) can affect us subtly, without us being aware of it. And then there are burglars, thunderstorms, car accidents, computer viruses, and rampaging mothers-in-law. (Okay, sorry—I didn't mean to freak you out. Please come out from behind the sofa.)

The good news is, as Witches, we have a little something extra we can use to protect ourselves from the bad stuff. (No, I said I'm not talking about those. Put that away.) I'm talking about protection magick.

Witches throughout history have made up charms and amulets to protect themselves and others from anything from drowning to the plague. (If that one worked, it was probably because the garlic kept anyone from getting close enough to infect you.) Today's Witches may not have to worry about the plague, but we still do magick to protect ourselves from whatever we feel threatens our safety or peace of mind.

I personally have a protection charm hung up by my front door, and I sprinkle a mix of protective herbs around the boundaries of my property every year or two. When I walk around scattering the herbal mixture, I visualize a line of white light protecting my property and repeat the following: "This land is protected, this house is protected, all who live within it are protected from any harm, intentional or unintentional, natural or manmade."

Protection magick often utilizes herbs and sea salt (the mix I mentioned above contains rosemary, sage, basil, and salt, in case you were wondering), black or white candles, black onyx, agate, or turquoise gemstones, and is done on a Sunday or a Tuesday. No matter what tools you use, remember that just because you did protection magick doesn't mean you shouldn't also use common sense to keep yourself safe: in other words, don't leave your car running with the keys in it and then get upset if someone steals it despite the great spell you put on it!

Charmed, I'm Sure:
"Protection Charm"

Here is a simple protection charm that can be hung over the front door, in your car, or even buried at the entrance to your house:

Take a black or white cloth (silk or cotton are best) and place in it a few sprigs of rosemary, some sage, a clove of garlic (still in its skin, if you don't want it to stink up the place), and some dried basil. Add a piece of black onyx or an agate, and tie up the whole bundle with black or white string. Visualize yourself safe and protected, along with whatever space you are trying to protect, then say the following words: "Safe for now, safe forever, harming none but harmed never."

Then place the charm wherever you feel it is needed.

PERFECT LOVE AND PERFECT TRUST

The Wiccan Rede tells us to abide with perfect love and perfect trust. What the heck does that mean, and can anybody really do it?

When we enter a sacred circle with our fellow Witches, we try to leave behind the petty squabbles and irritants of mundane life and come together with perfect love and perfect trust for each other. No worries about each other's little human imperfections or about our own. No self-consciousness about how we look (perhaps harder to pull off if you are practicing skyclad) or whether our voices are in tune during the chanting. Everyone working together as equals in the eyes of the god and goddess.

It sounds impossible, doesn't it? But the truth is, of all the "impossible" tasks that come our way as Witches—staying in focus when the phone rings in the middle of ritual, keeping our faith strong in the face of life's many nasty surprises, planning an outside ritual where it doesn't rain—this one turns out to be the easiest to achieve.

It doesn't happen every time, in every circle. But more times than not, when the circle is cast and we are in a place outside of time, something truly magickal happens. It is one of the facets of Witchcraft that is beyond description or explanation. But I have seen it happen, time after time, and it is truly an amazing experience.

All I can tell you is that I believe it is one of the gifts that comes with the practice of Witchcraft, and I encourage you (even if you are a Solitary most of the time) to find a group of fellow fliers and try it sometime.

Stand in that magickal circle and look at the shining faces of the people around you. Revel in the knowledge that here are folks who believe what you believe, who accept you for who you are without reservation or hesitation. Feel the presence of the gods within, and know that you are loved. Perfect.

Witch 101:
"Pantheon Pathways"

As Witches, we often draw upon the mythology of many different lands to find the god and goddess figures that we identify with most strongly. And while this can vary greatly from Witch to Witch (like everything else we do—hey, at least we are not a bunch of boring conformists), many of us are drawn to the pantheons (from the Greek "temple of the gods," meaning the officially recognized gods of a particular people) of the Greek, Roman, Egyptian, and Celtic cultures, with a few Norse and Hindu gods thrown in for good measure.

It is interesting to see how much the gods from one culture resemble the gods in another. It makes sense, I suppose, when you consider that most Pagan peoples had the same interests as we do today: love, protection, prosperity, the moon, growing things, etc.

In addition, it is historically possible in many cases to follow the path that a god took from one culture to another. For instance, many of the Roman gods and goddesses were taken more or less directly from the Greeks who preceded them.

It is fine to focus on one pantheon or culture, but it is also okay to mix and match. The gods that want you will find you, that much is for sure.

Witch Wit:
"Top 13 Reasons to Be a Pagan"

13. I enjoy the strange looks from the neighbors.

12. I'm a night person at heart.

11. We respect our elders...and our alders, willows, and oaks.

10. My church is my backyard.

9. We do more after midnight than most people do all day!

8. We're great with bonfires...as long as we're not on them.

7. We talk to dead people.

6. You live, you learn, you die, you forget. Then you come back...

5. Double the deities, double the fun!

4. We get more holidays.

3. Brooms get great mileage.

2. We were here first!

1. BELTANE!

Required Reading:
"Positive Magic"

There are a few books that I think all Witches should be required to read, and this is one of them: *Positive Magic* by Marion Weinstein. This great book is full of great facts on history, guidelines for ethics, and suggestions for using magick to improve yourself. Be sure to check out the chapter containing instructions for using words of power.

Quintessential Quotes:
"Prayer"

In Wicca, ritual is a framework in which prayer and magic take place. But prayer isn't solely a ritualistic act. We can pray at any time, and, utilizing our connections with the Goddess and God, contact Them for assistance and comfort.
— Scott Cunningham, *Living Wicca*

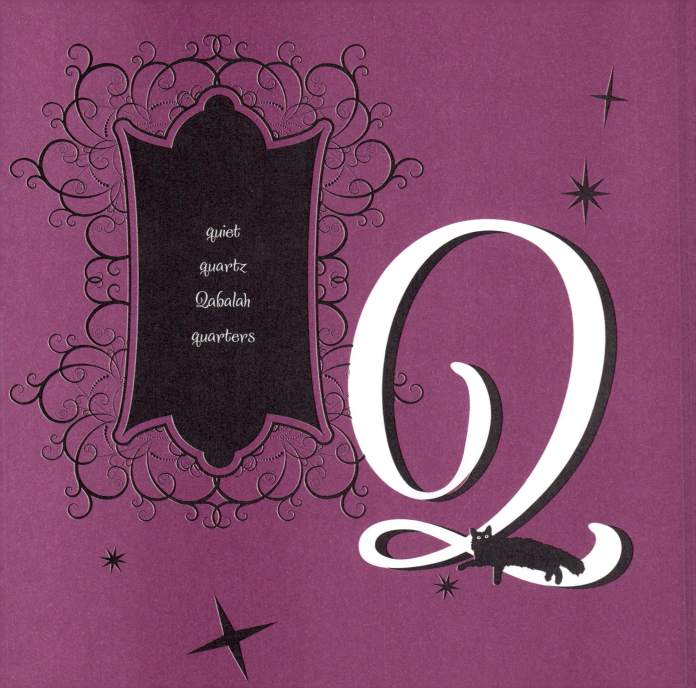

quiet

quartz

Qabalah

quarters

QUIET

We live in a noisy world. It seems like there is always some kind of sound in the background—television, radio, people talking, children playing, cars going by, lawn mowers, you name it. Even out in the country where I live (which tends to be considerably quieter than even the smallest city), there are trucks going by the house, tractors across the way, or some idiot down the street shooting off his gun just because he can. (Repeat after me: *I will not hex the neighbors, I will not hex the neighbors, I will not...*)

Sometimes it seems like there is so much noise it is hard to hear yourself think. And that's not a good thing, especially for a Witch.

We all want some peace and quiet occasionally, but for those of us who try (despite our often hectic lives) to pursue a spiritual path, it is a necessity—which doesn't, alas, make it any easier to find.

The truth is, we are not likely to stumble across a quiet moment accidentally—although when you do, I hope you grab it and appreciate it.

For most of us, having a few minutes of precious peace and quiet requires purposely creating a temporary oasis from the noise and commotion of our busy lives.

This may mean sitting in the bathtub with a few candles lit or retreating to the bedroom for half an hour with a book. Maybe you can take a half hour before anyone else in the house is awake to meditate or do yoga or just sit down with a cup of tea to think through the day to come.

However you do it, don't underestimate the importance of quiet. With so much going on around us, it is next to impossible to ponder weighty questions, make plans for the future, or concentrate enough to cast a spell.

Yet all those things are crucial to the practice of Witchcraft. So talk to the people who share your space and make them understand that the "do not disturb or else" sign means them, too. If you can, once or twice a week, get up early or stay up late to capture those quiet moments before and after everyone else is up and around and making noise. If you can't find quiet at home, then go to the park or the library. Do whatever it takes, but carve out the time in your busy schedule to devote a few minutes to you.

Because the gods aren't going to shout to be heard. You need to sit in silence and listen very, very carefully...

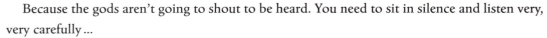

QUARTZ

Of all the stones used for magickal work, quartz is probably the most popular. Although quartz comes in many different forms, including rose quartz (pink), smoky quartz (grey), and green quartz (well, duh), the most popular type is clear, or crystal, quartz.

Crystal quartz has a long history of use by many varied shamanic and religious paths, including Native American. Because of its clarity, it is often associated with the power of water, but it also symbolizes the spirit and the intellect. Crystal quartz is one of the stones most commonly used to represent the goddess, and many Witches place a quartz crystal on their altars and use it during any lunar ritual.

Quartz has traditionally been used on top of staffs and wands, placed in power bags, and worn (usually coupled with silver) by shamans and high priestesses. The popular crystal ball used for scrying was sometimes made from a large piece of quartz (not the glass that is more common today) because of its ability to boost the psychic gifts of those who use it.

Crystal quartz is also used to promote dreams (again, to boost psychic ability in most cases), help bring peaceful sleep (and, yes, I would think it is hard to have both peaceful sleep and psychic dreams at the same time, but what do I know), create both protective and defensive magic, and in general to boost the power of any spell. Quartz also has strong healing properties, which probably explains some of its historical use by shamans.

Quartz is said to absorb negativity from the environment and can actually become dirty after prolonged or heavy use. To cleanse a quartz crystal, you can leave it out overnight under a full moon, wash it in running water (preferably something natural like rain or a stream, not the stuff that comes out of your tap—although that will work in a pinch), or waft it with either sage or sweetgrass.

If you use your quartz often, be sure to cleanse and purify it at least a couple times a year, or it may lose its oomph. If you stumble across a beautiful piece of quartz in your travels, remember that it makes a perfect gift for the witchy friends in your life. You can never have too much of this versatile and powerful stone.

Magic the Cat's Simple Spells:
"Quartz Quickie"

My Witch found this great little spell in Dorothy Morrison's book *Everyday Moon Magic:*[10]

ENERGY-INCREASING CHARM

Hold a small piece of quartz in your hand, and say:

Stone of power unsurpassed

By this spell that I now cast

Revitalize my body now

Energize it as I plow

Through all the things that I must do

Bring energy to my mind, too

So that I don't tire easily

As I will, so mote it be.

---

10 Page 175.

Qabalah

The Qabalah (also spelled Kabbalah, Kabala, and Cabala, in case you weren't confused enough by the first spelling) is a Jewish system of mysticism and philosophy that is said to have been around since before the time of Moses.

The word *Qabalah* (or Kabbalah, etc.) means "tradition" and is said to refer to the oral tradition of handing down knowledge from one generation to the next. The Qabalah has been studied by mystical scholars throughout the ages and was at its most popular during the Renaissance, when it was commonly used by magicians and alchemists.

The Qabalah is the basis for much of the magickal work done by the Golden Dawn, an order that included such well-known names as Aleister Crowley and A. E. Waite (of tarot fame).

Pagans today sometimes study the Qabalah because of the appeal of its Tree of Life, which provides a path whereby we can ascend to the divine while still alive.

There are many aspects of the Qabalah that some Pagans may find less than comfortable, including the emphasis on angels and other Christian ideas that were added on during the fifteenth century (can't leave anything alone, those people), but many Witches are intrigued by its long history and mystical view of the universe.

One of the fun aspects of being a Witch is that you can pick and choose from many paths and sources of information. No one can limit where you turn for knowledge and enlightenment. So if the Qabalah interests you, by all means add a book about it to the stack you have by your desk, your couch, and your bed. After all, it probably wouldn't still be around after all those years (since Noah!) if there wasn't something to it...

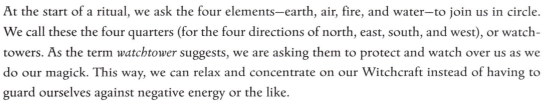

At the start of a ritual, we ask the four elements—earth, air, fire, and water—to join us in circle. We call these the four quarters (for the four directions of north, east, south, and west), or watch-towers. As the term *watchtower* suggests, we are asking them to protect and watch over us as we do our magick. This way, we can relax and concentrate on our Witchcraft instead of having to guard ourselves against negative energy or the like.

We also ask the watchtowers to lend us their assistance in our magickal work. As I mentioned in the section on elements (which, again, I know you have memorized), each element has certain aspects associated with it, such as air being the property that rules over intellect.

So, if you were going to do magick to help you succeed on an important test (in addition to studying hard, of course, not instead of studying at all), you might ask that quarter for particular help during your ritual.

Here is an example of a typical quarter call or invocation:

I call the watchtower of the north, the element of earth.

Come guard me in my circle, and keep me safe as I work my magickal craft.

Help me to stay grounded and centered, and lend me your strength.

Come now, and enter the circle. So mote it be.

Once we have completed our magickal work and are ready to open the circle, we dismiss the quarters. Don't be misled by the terms *calling* and *dismissing*—we don't actually try to boss the quarter powers around. After all, you don't want to irk the power of water and have your toilet explode, now do you?

Always invoke and dismiss the watchtowers respectfully, and say thank you when you are done. As Witches, we have the power to summon the elements, but hopefully we also have the wisdom to treat them with the awe and deference they deserve.

Helpful Hints:
"Quality vs. Quantity"

Keep in mind that it is more important to do a little magick well than to do a lot of magick poorly. If you only have an hour a month to devote to magickal work, you are better off taking that hour and really concentrating on what you want to achieve than you are trying to stuff a few minutes of magick into your day here and there and never really giving it enough attention to make it work.

ritual

rosemary

reincarnation

RITUAL

Ritual is a big part of being a Witch. So what is ritual, why do we do it, and how exactly is it done? I'm so glad you asked.

Essentially, ritual is a religious or spiritual ceremony, usually done in a more or less set fashion. And while what this entails differs from Witch to Witch and occasion to occasion (a private ritual for a full moon might be a lot less complicated than a large public gathering for Imbolc, for instance), Pagan rituals tend to contain some or all of the following elements:

- Cleansing and purification of the ritual space—this is usually done with some combination of sage (coming up under the *Ss* in case you want more info), incense, or salt and water.

- Calling of the quarters (which we talked a bit about under the elements entry).

- Invoking the goddess and/or the god.

- Casting the circle—this encloses the ritual space to protect those within as they work and also acts to contain the magickal energy.

- The actual magickal working (as we discussed in the entry on magick, which I know you also memorized), which can take a variety of forms.

- Grounding after the magick is done—often involving cakes and ale (food is good for bringing you back from the witchy realms to the everyday world).

- Dismissing the quarters.

- Thanking the goddess and the god.

- Opening the circle.

So that answers the "what" and the "how" questions, but what about "why?" Why go through all this fuss when you could just walk out into the woods and say, "Hey, Goddess, please could I have a new job, since my old one sucks?"

Well, the short answer is, you can—and many Witches do—skip the ritual and do just that. And depending on the circumstances, sometimes that is all that is needed.

But when you are working magick, the more you can focus your energy and your will, the more powerful your magick will be. Ritual helps us to focus by removing us from the distractions of our mundane lives, reminding us (with cues such as the smell of incense or the sound of drumming) that we are working magick, and concentrating our energies within the sacred space that we create within our circles.

All the elements of ritual, working together with our intent and our hearts, come together to make us more powerful Witches so that we can create the potent magick that we need to bring positive changes into our lives.

Ask Onyx:
"Right Ritual"

Dear Onyx,

I am a Solitary Witch and fairly new at all this. I have some books with rituals in them, and I have found a few more interesting rites online. How do I know which one to use?

Overwhelmed in Ohio

Dear Overwhelmed,

It's true that there is a lot of material out there for the new Witch to choose from, and that's a good thing—but it can be easy to get overwhelmed. The easiest way to resolve this is to pick the two or three that you like best (if you are doing a full moon ritual, for instance), and then just let your heart decide. Don't try to think it out, just go with the one that grabs you the most. If none of them grab you, then you either need to get different sources or—just maybe—simply light the candles and speak from your soul. The gods don't expect perfection, just your best effort, so don't worry too much about getting it "right."

Bright blessings,
Onyx

In the Witch's Tool Chest:
"Runes for Ritual"

At their simplest, runes are symbols carved or drawn onto some surface or other and most often used as divinatory tools. Many Witches have a set of rune stones. I have three: one set that I made myself out of clay as a project with my first group, one gemstone set that I bought, and my favorite, a beautiful set made out of dichroic glass by one of the members of Blue Moon Circle.

But runes can be used for more than predicting the future. Rune symbols have a power and an energy all their own, and this energy can be harnessed in magickal work as well. Try scratching a rune or two on a candle when casting a spell. Or use a wood-burning tool to etch some runes into your wooden staff or wand. Draw a rune on the paper you write a spell on or in your Book of Shadows.

There are a number of different symbols that you can use: the Norse and Germanic runes are most commonly known, but there are also Egyptian hieroglyphics, the Theban script alphabet, and a few others. Just pick the symbols that resonate with you, and add their energy to your magick.

Magic's Herbal Helpers:
"Roses Are Red"

Roses can be used for a number of magickal applications, including beauty, peace, sex, protection, and luck, but their most common use is in magick done for love. Rosebuds or petals can be added to sachets, charms, and bath mixtures, or you can burn rose incense during your ritual. Rose petals can even be baked into cookies to give to your beloved. (Be sure to take out the thorns first, though, or you may end up missing out on the kisses you crave.)

Roses also look beautiful on an altar, especially at Beltane or Midsummer. And if you want to get fancy, you can mix color magick and herbal magick, and pick the color of rose for the type of magick you want to work: yellow roses for intellectual love or to open up communication with the one you love; pink roses for friendship; red roses for passion...

And if you're a cat, they also make a tasty snack when your Witch leaves them out on the table. Mmm...good.

Rosemary is another all-around useful—and yummy-smelling—herb. Best known for its culinary uses (and if you don't think that rosemary chicken is magickal, then you haven't had mine), rosemary is easy to find and easy to grow, making it a perfect herb for the lazy Witch. (You know who you are.)

Besides making chicken tastier, rosemary has a number of magickal properties. It is primarily used in protection spells, sometimes combined with garlic (which is also good with chicken, but that's beside the point). I have a basic protection mix that I sprinkle around the outside of the house and the boundaries of my property once a year, the main component of which is rosemary. It can also be added to protection sachets and hung up over your altar or the entrance to your house.

If you want to have a simple form of protection that isn't obvious to Bob and Mary Mundane next door (you know the ones—they are always peering though their shades at the slightest whiff of burning sage), just plant a rosemary bush on either side of your front door.

Rosemary is also used for purification and is a traditional addition to the pre-ritual cleansing bath. If you don't have time for the whole bath, then soak some rosemary in water for a while and use the water to symbolically clean your hands before starting to work magick. Or stick a sprig of the herb in the container that you use for water during ritual.

Another of rosemary's magickal properties is a reflection of its use as a healing herb as well. In healing, rosemary is used to boost memory; when used magickally, it is said to aid the intellect. Either way, if you have an upcoming test or an important mental task (like, oh, I don't know...writing a book, perhaps), you can prepare yourself by having a cup of rosemary tea or putting a few drops of essential oil into a burner by your desk. Of course, if you have a test, studying might help too. (It's an herb, after all, not a miracle worker.)

You can find rosemary at any grocery store, although the dried stuff in the spice aisle is likely to be so old it might have been used by Druids at Stonehenge. If you can find the fresh herb in the produce section, that will work fine. Otherwise, your best bet is a health food store, New Age shop, or local garden center.

Or, of course, you can easily grow it yourself. Then you not only have it on hand for all your magickal work but also can grab a sprig or two the next time you want to whip up some truly magickal chicken!

REINCARNATION

Most Witches don't believe in heaven or hell (except here on earth, as in a really good piece of chocolate or a really bad date). Those are primarily Christian concepts.

What we do believe in is the ongoing cycle of birth, living, death, and rebirth. Like the cycle of the seasons that we call the Wheel of the Year, most of us view this cycle of life as a natural extension of our other spiritual beliefs.

Quintessential Quotes:
"Reincarnation"

However, each life is just that—new. There should be no dwelling on past lives, however fascinating it might seem to regress and discover the previous relationship. Get on with the present life and the present relationship. There are plenty of new lessons to be learned and new experiences to be had.

—Raymond Buckland, *Wicca for Life*

Since as Witches we believe in taking responsibility for our own actions, we also believe that we reap what we sow—that what you do in this life will determine what you end up dealing with in the next one.

Most Witches also believe that one of our major goals as human beings is to better ourselves (sometimes referred to as the Great Work, to acknowledge that for many of us this is a pretty big job...). Reincarnation means that, thankfully, we have more than one lifetime in which we can learn all that we need to know. (Personally, I'm sure that I will hit perfection any time now...the next lifetime, or maybe the one after that. Or the one after the one after that...oh, never mind.) The point is, we take what we are given in this particular incarnation and do the best we can with it.

Some Witches also believe in a place called the Summerlands, where we go to rest up in between lives and where we may meet up with our loved ones once again.

The main thing is, we don't view death as an end but merely as another transition, a natural step in an ongoing dance. While we mourn for those we will no longer have with us in this life, we also know that nothing in the universe is ever truly lost to us. We will see all those we have loved again sometime, either in the Summerlands or in another life.

Some Witches actively try to find out information about their past lives by using a variety of approaches, including psychics, trance work (also known as "journeying"), and past-life regression. And while many of the folks who offer such things are out-and-out frauds, there are some people out there who are the genuine article.

Just use some common sense if you are going to use outside help on your search. If someone tells you that you were Cleopatra or King James the something-or-other in another life, then asks you for lots of money, chances are good that the person in question is full of it.

Learning about a past life may help you to uncover the reasons for issues that you are dealing with in this one—especially if you seem to be stuck making the same mistakes over and over.

Hopefully, finding out more about who you were in a past life will help you work to improve the one you are living now.

Whether you seek to learn about your past lives or choose to focus exclusively on the here and now, the knowledge that what you do matters—not just today and tomorrow, but in many tomorrows to come—should inspire you to make the most out of the lessons that life, and the gods, offer you.

Stoned!
"Rose Quartz Rocks"

Rose quartz is used to encourage love and friendship, and it is said to open the heart chakra. It is also a great stone for encouraging feelings of calm and peacefulness. During a particularly stressful period in my life, I once spent an entire afternoon in a local New Age shop, picking up every medium-sized rose quartz crystal they had until I found the one that made me feel the calmest. Don't hesitate to keep looking until you find the stone that seems to resonate the best with your own inner energy.

Solitary

sage

Samhain

sex

spellcasting

sabbats

sacred space

SOLITARY

There are Witches who practice with a group and then there are the Solitaries. No, a Solitary isn't someone who is seriously antisocial and has too many cats (well... at least not always), it is just what we in the witchy world call someone who practices the Craft on his or her own. These folks are often referred to as Solitary practitioners, a term that always reminds me of someone in the medical field (Witch doctors, maybe?), but actually just means that the Witch in question practices alone.

So why do some Witches join a circle or coven while others do all or most of their magickal work by themselves?

Sometimes this is simply a matter of practical necessity—there may be no group close enough or no group that is willing to take on new members. Sometimes the only coven around is one in which there are folks who practice a different form of magick (traditional vs. eclectic, for example) or which includes someone the Solitary can't stand to be in the same room with, much less the same spiritual group. (If you can't find people to work with in perfect love and perfect trust, you're probably better off practicing alone, at least for now.)

Not everyone feels either the need or the desire to practice Witchcraft in the company of others. There are many Witches who prefer to pursue the Craft on their own, with little or no interaction with other Pagans. Some are too shy, too independent, or just not "group people." Some are drawn to a Solitary practice by the very nature of Solitary Witchcraft—quiet, peaceful, and highly individual.

Some Witches are simply more comfortable being Solitary, and there is a long tradition in the Craft of Witches who go it alone. There are certainly some benefits to a Solitary practice, which can be tailored to the preferences of the Witch doing it. It is in many ways both simpler and easier to be a Solitary Witch than to be a group one.

There is no right or wrong way to be a Witch. Whether you practice alone some of the time, all of the time, or only within a group setting, it is the practice itself that matters. If a Witch practices alone in the woods, does the goddess still hear him or her? You bet she does!

SAGE

Sage may be the most widely used magickal herb in the Pagan world—and that's really saying something, considering how many herbs we tend to use. (No, I'm not talking about *that* kind of herb.)

Although sage has a number of magickal properties, it is most commonly used to cleanse and purify a space or person before doing magickal work. The best kind of sage for smudging is white sage, which is sometimes found combined with other cleansing herbs like cedar or sweetgrass and tied up into a bundle called a smudge stick or wand. The top of this smudge stick is lit on fire (as you would the top of a stick of incense) and then gently wafted around the area to be cleansed. (Note: sometimes bits of burning herb fly off and alight on the altar, floor, or clothing—be prepared!)

I have found this to be particularly useful when people first gather in circle to do group magick, especially if anyone (or everyone, as is usually the case with my bunch of Witches) is feeling particularly frazzled or stressed.

My group, Blue Moon Circle, always starts out each ritual by passing a small sage wand around the circle so that everyone can smudge himself or herself. Most people begin at the top of their heads and then slowly move the sage wand down their bodies, paying particular attention to any spot that feels especially in need of cleansing (head or heart, for instance).

In some group rituals, it is common practice for one of the participants to walk around the outside of the circle and smudge everyone taking part (sometimes using a large feather to waft the smoke inward, which can be quite beautiful to see).

Smudging done in this fashion helps to quiet the mind and spirit while also washing away whatever negativity we might be carrying in from the mundane world. When this practice is done on a regular basis, the smell alone serves as a subconscious cue that tells us it is time to relax and focus on magick.

Sage can also be used to smudge an entire room or house if necessary. The little farmhouse where I live is over 100 years old and undoubtedly contains a lot of history I know nothing about. So before I moved in a single piece of furniture (but after I painted over the pink walls), I gathered together the group of Witches that I was practicing with at the time and we did a house cleansing and blessing.

Sage also has a number of traditional magickal properties and is useful in spells for healing, prosperity, and energy. In addition, it is a tasty culinary herb, although in this case you are better off using regular garden sage rather than the white sage you find in smudge sticks.

The word *sage* means "wise," and the word *Wicca* is said by some to come from the Latin for "wise one"—so be a wise Witch, and go get some sage!

Magic the Cat's Simple Spells:
"Sage Advice for House Cleansing"

This is a fairly simple procedure and one that my Witch recommends to anyone who moves into a new home, whether it is a house, an apartment, or an old VW bus. You can do this alone or with a bunch of witchy friends (in which case you might as well get food and wine for afterwards and call it a party) and with as much or as little ceremony as you desire.

Simply open all the windows to give the negative energy a place to get out (if it is freezing out, you can skip this step or open and close each window as you go), then start at the bottom of the house and move up. Move through each room, smudging as you go, with particular attention given to any openings (doors, windows, chimneys, etc.). If you want a little extra oomph, you can sprinkle sea salt or a mixture of salt and water in the corners and on the windowsills. When you are done, you can ask the gods to bless and guard your new home and keep all within it safe.

Remember as you walk through all the spaces of your home to concentrate on driving away any negative energy and leaving clean, fresh rooms behind you. This can also be done in any house where there has been a crisis or a big fight, anything that would cause a sudden upsurge in nasty energy, or even once or twice a year for a kind of spiritual spring-cleaning.

One note of warning: burning sage smells a whole lot like pot (or so I'm told, since I wouldn't possibly know what pot smells like, being a "just say no" kind of cat...tee hee), so you may want to be cautious about using it in public spaces...

SAMHAIN

This holiday has always seemed to me to represent all that is witchy and wonderful. Unlike its counterpart, the festive and joyous Beltane, Samhain is a solemn occasion, quieter and more thoughtful (although still a lot of fun in its own way).

Samhain (pronounced SOW-wen 'cause it's Celtic, and nothing Celtic is ever pronounced the way it is spelled) falls on October 31 and is also known as the Witches' New Year. This is the Pagan holiday that provided the origins for the Christian holiday of All Hallows Eve, which in turn became known as Halloween.

Many of Halloween's traditions can be traced back to its Pagan roots. Samhain is said to be the night of the year when the veil between the worlds is thinnest. Some believe that it is on this night that all those who have died in the previous year pass over to the other side and all those who will be born in the coming year cross over to join the living.

We take this time to say our final farewells to all those whom we have lost in the year gone by and to remember our ancestors with stories and remembrances. You can easily see where Halloween got its ghosts and ghouls from—although we're Witches, so we ain't afraid of no ghosts.

At Samhain, the goddess is honored in her role as crone, growing older as the year grows colder. She mourns the loss of her consort, who willingly sacrificed himself at Mabon. But she also looks forward to the birth of the infant god at Yule. (And if you're wondering how a crone can be pregnant—well, she's a goddess, after all.)

Samhain is a holiday that perfectly reflects both the light and dark aspects of the Pagan world—while we acknowledge sorrow for what we have lost, we also celebrate that which is to come and look forward to the gifts that a new year might bring. For let us not forget that Samhain is also the third of the harvest festivals and a time for rejoicing as well.

So let the bonfire blaze against the night sky and light a candle to honor those who have gone before. Chant, drum, or pray in silence. Gather with the largest group of Witches you can find, or walk the woods alone with only the shadow of an old woman to keep you company. But however you choose to observe this most witchy of holidays, don't forget to look with joy and anticipation toward the year to come, and thank the gods that on this day of all days, you are a Witch.

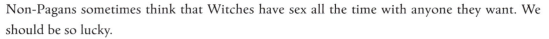

Sex

Non-Pagans sometimes think that Witches have sex all the time with anyone they want. We should be so lucky.

But it is true that sex can be used as a component of magick. When it is, it is taken as seriously as any other form of magickal work, if not more so, because it can be very powerful. Traditionally the Great Rite was when a high priest and high priestess had sex as a way of enacting the sacred marriage of the god and goddess. This was usually done as part of a sabbat celebration.

On a more personal level, any Witch can use sex as a part of ritual, as long as he or she can maintain the necessary focus, has a willing partner, and approaches the act with reverence and love. The traditional method for doing sex magick is to prepare all the ingredients for your spell and then cast the circle wherever you will be, um…practicing.

Once your spell is readied, you and your partner will start to slowly build energy by kissing, caressing, and doing that voodoo that you do so well. The slower and more mindful you are, the more power you will raise for your spell. The trick here is keeping at least part of your mind focused on the spell while you are being distracted by the act of sex. (And if you're not at least a little distracted, you're not doing it right!)

At the culmination of the act (you know what I mean, don't make me spell it out), you and your partner release the energy into the spell and send it out into the universe.

Then open the circle and have a snack. Personally, I like cold pasta, but cakes and ale works too.

Spellcasting

As Witches, we often use a variety of tools to help us with our craft. Not only is this traditional and practical (tools often help us focus our energy), but it can be a lot of fun as well. There is nothing like finding the perfect athame or lighting a bunch of beautiful candles to help us get in touch with our joyous inner Witch.

But the truth is, none of these things are necessary for the successful casting of spells. Helpful and fun maybe, but not necessary. To practice spellcasting, there is really only one thing that you need and that is intent. In other words, in order to create magick, you have to *want* to create magick. Yup, it's really that simple. Seriously.

Of course, just because something is simple doesn't mean that it is easy—or at least not as easy as it sounds. One cannot just sit down on the couch and say, "Hey, presto, I'm doing magick," and have it be so (unless you are going to pull a rabbit out of your sleeve, but that is a different kind of magic and not my area of expertise at all).

Intent is essentially a matter of focus, and willpower, and certainty. What the heck am I talking about, you ask? I'll give you an example.

Suppose that you decide you want to do some prosperity magick. Unless you're a Rockefeller, most of us will have a time or two when we could use a little extra money. Or a lot of extra money. Either way, you can gather up some green candles, make up some money-drawing magickal oil, and perform your ritual on a Thursday. But with or without these tools, you will want to do the following before you actually cast your spell:

Decide what it is you want—This is the true intent of your spell. Do you want enough money to pay the electric bill that is due next Tuesday? Do you want a specific new job? Do you want to win the lottery? (Yeah, well, who doesn't? If I were you, I'd aim for something a bit more likely. Nobody likes a greedy Witch.) Prosperity means a lot of things to different people. Make sure that you know what you are asking the gods to bring you.

Then, focus on your goal—In this case, you may want to visualize yourself writing out that bill or getting a phone call telling you that you've gotten the job you wanted or going to the bank to deposit money into your account. Be practical and reasonable, but don't be afraid to visualize the best-case scenario for your situation.

Now, believe that it is possible—I know, this is a tricky one. Most of us have that little doubting voice in the back of our heads whispering unhelpful stuff like "I can't do it," "Why would the gods help me," or "Maybe magick doesn't really work." Just tell the darned voices to shut up for once and focus the best you can anyway. Take a few minutes to really believe: believe in yourself; believe in the infinite possibilities of the universe; believe in the gods and the power of magick. Remember that time is an illusion and that in some place/time/reality, the prosperity that you wish for has already come to pass.

Now and only now are you ready to cast your spell—The candles you use may help you focus, but your intent and your will to make it happen are what truly give your spell power. Intent is what magick is really all about.

Oh, and good luck with that lottery thing. Be sure and let me know if you win…

Sabbats

Sabbats are the eight major holidays of the Pagan calendar; the eight spokes on the Wheel of the Year, so to speak. I talk about each one in detail throughout the rest of the book, but here is the quick and simple review version, for those who need it:

Samhain—October 31 (Halloween). Known as the Witches' New Year, both the beginning and the end of the year. Last harvest festival.

Yule—December 21 (approx.). The Winter Solstice. Celebrations and gift giving during the longest night of the year. The origin of Christmas.

Imbolc—February 2. Celebrates the first hints of spring. The origin of Groundhog Day.

Ostara—March 21 (approx.). The Spring Equinox. Celebrates the arrival of spring. The origin of Easter.

Beltane—May 1 (May Day). Sometimes celebrated starting April 30. Fertility festival.

Midsummer—June 21 (approx.). The Summer Solstice and the longest day of the year.

Lammas—August 1. Also known as Lughnasadh. First harvest festival.

Mabon—September 21 (approx.). The Autumnal Equinox and second harvest festival.

Not all Witches celebrate all the sabbats, but many do. They are a time to celebrate the blessings in our lives and observe the cycle of the seasons.

Quintessential Quotes:
" Sacred Space"

Wiccans can transform their living rooms and bedrooms into places of power. They do this by creating sacred space, a magical environment in which the Deities are welcomed and celebrated, and in which Wiccans become newly aware of the aspects of the God and Goddess within.

—Scott Cunningham, *Wicca*

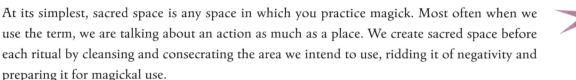

SACRED SPACE

At its simplest, sacred space is any space in which you practice magick. Most often when we use the term, we are talking about an action as much as a place. We create sacred space before each ritual by cleansing and consecrating the area we intend to use, ridding it of negativity and preparing it for magickal use.

Although Witches may have permanent places in which they practice (like the stone circle behind my barn, for instance), in essence we can create holy ground anywhere we want, at any time. Heck, we're Witches—all ground is holy, really. We don't need a church or any other structure that is dedicated to only sacred use; any living room will do, as long as we take a few vital steps before beginning our work.

Sacred space is created by delineating the area in which we intend to work, usually by marking the circle with chalk, yarn, candles, or stones, or simply by having a group of Witches standing around in a more-or-less circular fashion. (The larger the group, the less actually circular it tends to be!)

The area is then cleansed of any unwanted energies, often by burning sage or incense and sprinkling salt and/or water. There is no one right way to do this, but most Witches eventually find a form of cleansing they are comfortable with and use it more or less consistently.

The circle is then cast, and you are in sacred space. It really is that simple. But don't be misled—just because it is simple doesn't make it any less important. Creating sacred space is an important part of any formal witchy ritual; without it, you are vulnerable to outside energies, and the energy you are trying to build inside the circle will likely waft away before you can do anything magickal with it.

Elemental Essentials:
"Speaking Stick"

The speaking stick is not a tool, exactly. In fact, it doesn't even have to be a stick. (Confused yet?) The speaking stick is an object that is passed around the circle at the end of many group rituals. As it goes around, each person has a chance to speak uninterrupted for a few moments, and everyone else in the circle simply listens. It is a time for words that come from the heart and calm acceptance. It can be amazingly moving and empowering. (How often in your day-to-day life does anyone actually stop and truly listen to what you have to say?) The speaking stick can be an actual stick or it can be a large feather, a stone, a shell, or anything else that can be passed from person to person. What is important is that everyone respects the "stick" and what it symbolizes—a moment out of time for each Witch to speak and be heard.

Food of the Gods:
"Seeds"

Sunflower seeds, pumpkin seeds…these are not just great, healthy additions to a salad or to sprinkle on top of homemade bread (although there's that, too). Seeds are a symbol of rebirth, since each seed contains the potential for growth. They are also good for energy work, since they each hold the potential energy of the plant that might someday come from them. Use seeds in rituals and in food for feasts, especially during the spring and early summer.

Required Reading:
"The Spiral Dance"

Almost every Witch who has been practicing the Craft for more than a few months has heard of *The Spiral Dance: A Rebirth of the Ancient Religion of the Great Goddess* by Starhawk. This must-read book, currently out in a twentieth-anniversary edition, contains rituals, invocations, exercises, and magick. But more than that, it contains the wisdom of a woman who has been a leader in the Neopagan movement for many years. Run, do not walk, to get this book.

tea

teaching

tools

Threefold Law

trees

Tea

Some of the best magick is also the simplest. Take tea, for instance. The Japanese make a ritual of preparing the perfect pot of green tea because they understand the power of mixing herbs and ceremony. And while the Japanese might design their ritual to achieve a calm oasis in a hectic day, Witches can combine herbs with magickal lore and focused intent to create teas that are a powerful magick in their own right.

Obviously, not all herbs are equally suited to making a magickal tea. I wouldn't advise, for instance, a nice steaming cup of deadly nightshade tea, charming though that may sound. (And no, you can't serve it to your mother-in-law either; remember, harm none.)

But there are plenty of herbs you may think of as traditional herbal teas that also have magickal properties you can take advantage of by adding a little ritual to your daily tea ceremony.

So how do you take plain old herbal tea and make it magickal? Simple, really. As with other magickal uses of herbs, if at all possible use the fresh plant. If you must use dried, try to get it from a good source.

Then, heat your water and fix your magickal goal firmly in your mind. You may want to mix more than one herb (bergamot and ginger for prosperity, for instance) to increase the power of your magick or recite a spell to give it extra oomph. If possible, use a pretty teapot or mug. Place your herbs in a tea ball or loose in your container, and slowly pour the water over them. As the herbs steep, concentrate on your goal and envision the steam from the water carrying your intentions up to the gods.

Finally, drink your tea slowly and thoughtfully while focusing all your intent on whatever it is you hope to achieve.

(And don't forget about that other magickal use of tea: the reading of tea leaves for divination. I see great things in your future ...)

Magic's Herbal Helpers:
"Ten Terrific Teas"

Here are ten of the herbs that I recommend for use in magickal teas. They are all easy to find and taste good, too! (Of course, my favorite is catnip. What's yours?)

Bergamot—Use for prosperity, peace, and restful sleep. Hint: bergamot is what flavors Earl Grey tea.

Catnip—Not just for Fluffy, catnip can be used for love, luck, and peace. It is also used medicinally to help with sleep, but you will probably have to fight your familiar for it, which will undoubtedly wake you right back up again.

Chamomile—Use for prosperity, meditation, peace, and sleep. Also good for settling an upset tummy—just ask Peter Rabbit...

Dandelion—Use to aid in divination and calling spirits. And no, dandelion wine is not the same as dandelion tea...although if you drank enough of it you would probably see all sorts of spirits.

Elderberry—Use for prosperity and protection, especially against negative forces. It also is great when you are fighting a cold, a negative force if I ever saw one.

Ginger—Use for prosperity, power, success, love, energy, courage, and sex magick. The Chinese consider ginger to be a "heating" herb, as opposed to a "cooling" one, and you can see how this would translate into all its magickal uses. Ginger is also used medicinally for digestive upset and to treat colds.

Lemon—Use for purification, to help boost energy, and in healing. You can use dried lemon peel or just squeeze the juice from a fresh lemon into hot water. It has lots of vitamin C, which helps with healing, and is often added to cleaning solutions because of its ability to purify and cleanse.

Lemon balm—Use for purification, prosperity, and peace. Decorative and easy to grow—as the name *balm*, which means "soothing," would indicate—this plant is used medicinally to calm and ease sleep. Lemon balm is a native Mediterranean herb dedicated to the goddess Diana.

Peppermint—Use for love, lust, energy, and purification and as a mental stimulant.

Rose—Use for love, beauty, psychic power, protection, peace, and sex. Rose tea is usually made from rosehips, which are the fruit of the rose bush (and high in vitamin C). You can also use the petals.

These are just a small sampling of the many herbs that can be made into magickal teas; there are literally hundreds more that can be used (although not all of them will taste as good as those listed above—sage tea, for instance, tastes just awful). Keep in mind that not all herbs are safe to take internally, and that even those that are might cause an allergic reaction if you are the sensitive type. If you're not certain of an herb's safety, do your research first, drink second. Also, use caution if you are collecting herbs in the wild—some perfectly safe herbs look an awful lot like their poisonous cousins. And be sure to save some catnip for me!

Magic the Cat's Simple Spells:
"Tea and Tarot"

If you want to do a simple spell for tea-leaf reading or to boost your vision before doing a tarot reading (or any other kind of divination), brew a cup of tea and say the following before drinking it:

In this cup of steaming tea
Show me what I need to see.

In the Witch's Tool Chest:
"Tarot Travels"

Tarot cards are another great tool for divination and personal transformation. Usually a deck consisting of 78 cards, 22 major arcana and 56 minor arcana, the tarot dates back to the eighteenth century and has long been popular with those involved in the mystical arts.

The tarot has a long history of use by Witches, who employ it to open their minds to the higher plane and access wisdom and knowledge that might not normally be available to them. Although primarily used for divination purposes (in her book *The Spiral Dance*, Starhawk talks about consulting the cards to discover the direction that Witchcraft would take over the coming years[11]), Witches also use images from the tarot for meditation, spiritual journeys, and symbols for magickal work.

There are many beautiful decks out there these days, including one called *The Witches Tarot*. All you have to do is pick the one that appeals to you most and then let your mind wander wherever the cards take it.

11 Starhawk, *The Spiral Dance*, 16.

If anyone asked you to list some of the more important aspects of being a Witch, teaching might not be one of the things that comes to mind. But it should be.

Yes, it is important to respect our connection to nature and to worship the Old Gods. Yes, we should follow the paths laid down by the Pagans who preceded us while also setting out on our own new roads to wisdom, knowledge, and self-improvement.

But very little of this is possible without at least a little help from those who have preceded us on the path and who are willing to help show us the way.

If you are a Solitary Witch, you may think that you got where you are without any help. Nobody taught you, right? You learned it all on your own. How? Oh, you read books…and who wrote those books? Ah, that's right—teachers.

No matter where you learned your witchy knowledge—whether it was from your high priestess and high priest in a coven, a fellow witchy friend, or just a bunch of books that you read while no one was looking—*someone* took the time and energy to teach you.

Some Witch somewhere said, "This knowledge is important; I need to share it," and set aside the tasks of living and being a Witch long enough to write it down, pass it down orally, or do whatever it took to make sure that someone somewhere knew that particular spell, ritual, or bit of ancient lore.

Ironically, much of our history was lost because those who would have been the teachers for the next generation were killed or sent into hiding. *We must make sure that this never happens again.* It is up to us to teach each other and the next generation, to ensure that our own knowledge is handed on to other Witches so that it can never again be lost in the fog of hatred, fear, and ignorance.

We are all the teachers now. You don't have to be a coven elder with twenty years' experience to have something worth teaching. Each of us knows something worth sharing.

In my circle, we take turns doing the teaching. As the high priestess, I may do more than the others, but each member of my circle has some area in which they know more than I do. I am as happy to learn as I am to teach.

For each thing that I learn, I can then pass that on to another Witch, and another, and another. Much of the information that is contained in the book you hold in your hands was once the gift of some other teacher. So take the time to learn and to share that knowledge with other Witches (and even a mundane or two). Because knowledge is power, and we as Witches must never let that power be taken away from us again.

TOOLS

As Witches, we practice the Craft. And like any good craftsperson, most of us use tools to help us with our work. Of course in our case, the work is magickal and so are many of the tools, but that's beside the point.

Are tools strictly necessary? No, of course they're not. One can be a Witch with nothing more than hands and heart and mind. But in many cases, tools make our work easier—not to mention that they're cool and fun, too!

Witchy tools are used for a number of different purposes. Some of them are specifically intended to direct energy, aid in divination, or add power to our spells. In addition, the use of tools helps us to focus on the magickal task at hand: for instance, lighting a candle to focus attention on a spell or goal.

So what are some of the most common magickal tools and their uses? Most Witches have some or all of the following:

Athame—A ritual knife, usually double-sided; represents the male.

Boline—A curved knife used for cutting, often to harvest herbs that will be used magickally.

Candles—These come in all different shapes, sizes, and colors, and are used for a number of varied purposes.

Incense—Incense is used to cleanse an area or represent air on the altar.

Sage—Sage smudge sticks are used to purify and cleanse a space (or a Witch).

Tarot cards, runes stones, scrying mirrors, etc.—All these tools are used to help boost and focus psychic ability for the purpose of divination.

Herbs—Herbs are used in a number of forms, including magickal oils, tinctures, teas, incenses, charm bags, and more.

Salt—Salt is used to purify and to represent earth on the altar (sea salt is best).

Water—Used with salt to purify and cleanse, represents water on the altar. (I know, you wouldn't usually think of water as a tool, but if you are making up a list of supplies that you will need for a ritual and leave this one off, you will feel pretty silly when you reach for it and it isn't there.)

Broom—A traditional symbol of the Witch, it is used to sweep away negativity and clear a space before using it for rituals.

Book of Shadows—This is the book in which Witches record spells, recipes, and all the other information that we use to work our craft.

Books, books, books—In addition to a Book of Shadows, most Witches have shelf after shelf filled with all sorts of reference books, from herbal manuals to Pagan history. These books are as much a part of the witchy toolbox as an athame or a broom, and in some ways they are more valuable. Besides, we just love 'em. Books—good!

Cauldron—Represents the womb of the goddess, usually made of metal or pottery and used on the altar to burn things in or for mixing magickal ingredients.

Chalice—A cup or goblet (also represents the female), used to hold the ale for cakes and ale or any wine to be used as a libation during a ritual.

Wand—Usually made of wood, like an athame, a wand is used to point and direct energy.

Drums, flutes, and other musical instruments—Drums especially are used for raising energy or creating a meditative mood in circle.

Optional—Crystals, flowers, or anything else that you find useful.

In the end, a tool is merely that—something that you make use of because it helps you in your craft. Be careful not to load yourself down with so many that they get in your way instead of making things easier. Other than that, just have fun with them.

It doesn't matter where you get them (as long as the source is positive), how many you have, or whether or not you use them often. As long as they aid you in your craft, tools are a beautiful and enjoyable part of being a Witch.

THREEFOLD LAW

Karma, in essence, is a matter of cause and effect. You know the sayings: What goes around comes around. You reap what you sow. If you keep scowling, your face will end up freezing like that. (No, wait, that last one was from my mother.) You get the idea, anyway.

Witches take it one step further and call it the threefold law, or the law of three. In short, whatever you put out into the universe comes back to you times three.

So if you are kind and loving to others, you will receive even more love in return. On the other hand, if you are grumpy, cranky, nasty, or any of those other dark-side dwarves, you will reap more of the same. Not so pleasant, really.

If you give this some thought, you will realize that this Pagan "rule" pretty much takes the fun out of the whole idea of the Wicked Witch. Fairy tales aside, there are not too many Witches who would risk the consequences that come from serious nastiness.

Just think about it: you decide to cast a spell to give your ex-boyfriend's new gal pal pimples before their next big date, only to end up with a major case of hives on parts of your body you don't want to mention. (Oh, yes, it really does work that way—trust me.) No self-respecting Witch messes with the threefold law, believe you me.

Does this mean that there are no Witches out there who do negative magick? Sadly, no. But every religion has folks who talk the talk but don't walk the walk, and that includes us. (Right, like you've never met a Christian who lied, stole, or coveted his neighbor's wife/riding lawn-mower/SUV.)

There are always people who think that the rules don't apply to them or that they will some-how escape the consequences of their actions. But rest assured, eventually karma comes up and bites them on the butt. (Three times. How much is that going to hurt?)

What it comes down to is that Witches believe strongly in personal responsibility. What you put out there is what you will get back.

So if you don't like what life is dishing out to you, you might want to think about ways in which you can improve your interactions with others, your view of yourself, and your general mindset. If you focus on putting out as much good stuff as possible, you may be amazed by what comes back to you … times three.

Dear Onyx,

I realize that as Witches we are not supposed to harm anyone, and the threefold law says that whatever we put out, we get back times three—but what about really bad people, like child abusers and terrorists? Can we hex them? Wouldn't that be using our power for the good of all?

Perplexed About the Hex

Dear Perplexed,

This is a tricky one, and not all Witches agree about the answer. In general, though, I have to think that doing anything to harm someone purposely is a bad idea. The problem is, once you decide you can say who is "good" and who is "bad," where do you draw the line? I am much more comfortable with the idea of using a binding spell if you feel that you are truly in danger. This binds someone from doing harm but does not interfere in his or her free will in any other way. And, to be honest, even this is a slippery slope. When in doubt, I'd stick to defensive magick and leave the big judgments to the gods.

Bright blessings,
Onyx

TREES

Trees have been considered mystical, powerful, and sacred in cultures throughout history. They played an important part in magickal work for everyone from the Greeks to the Druids, both of whom worshipped in sacred groves, and have often been linked to specific gods. Witches use trees in various ways, including wands, broom handles, and spell ingredients, and if anyone calls us tree huggers, they're likely to be more right than they know!

Various trees have different magickal associations. Here are a few of the ones most often used in magick:

Apple—Associated with Diana, Apollo, Venus, and Athena; used for love and healing. Good for wands.

Ash—Associated with Poseidon, Thor, and Mars; used for protection, healing, and water rituals. A good wood for wands or broom handles.

Elder—Associated with Venus; used for purification, love, and protection. Another good wand wood.

Hawthorn—Used for protection, associated with Witches in England.

Hazel—Associated with Diana, Thor, Artemis, and Mercury; used for protection, fertility, and to increase mental abilities. A good wood for wands and divining rods.

Pine—Associated with Dionysus, Pan, Venus, and Cybele; used for fertility and purification. When doing magick outside, use a pine bough as a broom to sweep your circle space clear of negativity.

Rowan—Associated with Thor; used for protection and healing. Good for magic wands and divining rods.

Willow—Associated with Hecate, Persephone, Ceres, Artemis, and Mercury; used for healing and wishes. This is one of the witchiest trees there is, and it's referred to by Witches as the "Tree of Enchantment" and used with moon magick. Another good wood for wands, especially those used for healing.

If you are lucky enough to have trees on your property, be sure to spend some time sitting under one and communing with its spirit. If not, feel free to go to a park and hug one anyway. If anyone asks, just tell them you are talking to your mother!

Witch 101:
"Trances"

Witches have historically used trances as a tool for divination, astral travel, self-exploration, healing, and to speak to the gods. While trance work is something that is best approached with caution, there are some simple ways to enter into an altered state of consciousness without worrying about getting in over your head (so to speak). The simplest of these is meditation.

Find a quiet place and get comfortable, either sitting or lying down. Slowly bring your awareness to your breathing, counting your breaths if that helps. Hear the sounds around you as background noise and focus on the space between your brows called the third eye. See it glow with light, and open yourself to any information that the universe may send. If you are new at this, you may wish to begin by casting a protective circle or envisioning yourself surrounded by protective light, just in case. (Open is open, after all.) Don't expect much on the first try—trance work is something that improves with practice.

218

Ask Magic the Cat:
"Tiger's-eye Tales"

Dear Magic the Cat,

I am a Witch who is just starting out. I am looking for a good gemstone to use for courage and confidence, and my familiar, Spooky, suggested that a magickal cat would know all about such things. Can you suggest a stone for me?

Wimpy Witch in Wyoming

Dear Wimpy,

Everybody needs a boost in confidence from time to time (well, not cats, of course). Try my favorite stone, tiger's-eye. Tiger's-eye is a mottled brown earth stone that is good for both of the magickal uses you want, as well as protection, prosperity, luck, and power. It helps increase energy flow, so it can be especially useful when you are sick—or if you are trying to keep up with Spooky.

Familiarly,
Magic the Cat

Great Gods!
"A Sight for Thor Eyes"

If you like your gods larger than life and heroic, take a look at Thor, the Norse god of thunder. Thor is often described as a huge, red-bearded champion who wields a magickal hammer named Mjollnir, capable of creating thunder and throwing lightning bolts.

As you might imagine, Thor is a sky god, as well as a god of war, storms, sea journeys, and justice. (I'm thinking the hammer comes in handy for that. Haven't you ever just wanted to thump someone who you knew was in need of a little not-so-gentle justice?)

Thor was originally worshipped from the Viking period (around 700 AD) well into the Christian era, and he was the defender of Asgard, the home of the Norse gods.

unity

urban Witch

universal

U

Unity

William Shakespeare wrote, "What's in a name? That which we call a rose by any other name would smell as sweet."

So does it matter if you call yourself a Wiccan, a Pagan, a Green Witch, a Gardnerian, or any of the other myriad names we use to say we are Witches? The issue of "name" is a source of ongoing debate in the Pagan community.

Personally, I call myself a Wiccan. There are a number of reasons for this: it seems to me to be a name that most people recognize, so that they have at least a clue as to what I am talking about when I use it; I like the idea of a word that may have come from the Old English *wicce* and *wicca*, meaning one who divines or casts spells; and it so happened that my first teacher and high priestess used that term, so that is what I learned to call myself.

(None of these things may apply to you, of course, and I am sure that you have your own reasons for using whichever name it is that you have chosen to call yourself, all of which are as reasonable, or as gut-feeling-right, as mine.)

But do I think that it really matters whether I call myself Pagan, Wiccan, Witch, or "slightly strange woman who worships the Old Gods and has too many cats"? No, I don't.

I know many folks who insist (often and loudly) that they be called Pagan but not Witch, or Witch but not Wiccan. And certainly I believe that each of us should use the name with which we are the most comfortable.

But I wish—and this is just me, now—but I really wish that witchy folks wouldn't make such a big deal about this. I swear, if I hear one more Pagan say, "Oh, I'm not a Wiccan, I'm a Witch," I'm going to scream. Loudly.

Because the hard truth is, no matter what you call yourself, there are a lot more of them than there are of us, whatever the name. And while I will fight with my last breath for your right to call yourself any name you like, I think that we would be a lot better off using our energy for other things.

What it comes down to, I believe, is that we—Pagans, Wiccans, Witches, or whatever—have a lot more in common than we have differences, and we need to remember that and stick together. We need to pay a little more attention to the aspects of who and what we are that bring us together and a little less to those that keep us apart.

In the end, the names that we call ourselves don't matter. All Witches are our brothers and sisters, our mothers and fathers, our friends and our teachers. No matter how different, we are still the same.

And whoever we are and whatever we call ourselves, we need to stand together in unity. Now *that* would really be sweet.

Urban Witch

The witchy world revolves around nature. Paganism in all its forms is a nature-based religion, and Witches try whenever possible to use materials from the natural world (like herbs, stones, etc.) and celebrate rituals in the great outdoors. There are probably at least four or five times in this book alone where I tell you to grow your own herbs if you can.

But what if you are an urban Witch living in the middle of a concrete jungle and not a country Witch living in the woods? Does this mean that you are any less of a Witch?

Of course not. (Well, you knew I was going to say that, didn't you? Don't be silly.) These days, I am happily ensconced in my country farmhouse about six miles outside of town—and I have never been one to live in real cities like NYC or LA—but when I started my practice of Wicca, I lived right smack in the middle of a small city, Oneonta (pop. 10,000 to 20,000, depending on whether the colleges are in session or not). My high priestess lived a few blocks from me, also in the city.

We did hold some of our rituals inside, mostly because of weather (winters are nasty here). But we often met outside as well, sometimes in her backyard, sometimes at someone else's house, and sometimes in a local park. Her backyard was sheltered on three sides, but people could walk past on the other side. The parks were open to the public.

You would think that this would have caused a problem, but in truth, it never did. We would sometimes get curious looks as people strolled by and noticed a group of strangely dressed folks standing in a circle, but no one ever bothered us. Then there was the famous incident of the Samhain ritual in the park that was attended by about thirty Witches and one uniformed bicycle cop who stopped by to see what the heck we were up to there in the dark.

Obviously, if you live in a large city (like New York) it may be harder to hold a ritual in a public space, but I am guessing that you can always find some outside spot if you look hard enough. You may not be able to light up a big bonfire or drum really loudly, but there should be a patch of greenery you can use with some reasonable limitations.

There is also nothing wrong with holding all your rituals inside if you have no other choice. As I said, much of the year where I live, we are driven inside by either snow or torrential rains or bloodthirsty, man-and-woman-eating mosquitoes. You just do the best you can.

If you can't be outside, bring some of the outside in. Decorate your altar with flowers and stones, feathers, and shells. Focus on the fact that, no matter how far up in a building you are, somewhere underneath you still lies Mother Earth and somewhere overhead the moon still shines. Grow your herbs on a sunny windowsill or buy them fresh at a farmers' market.

No matter where you practice your craft, it is your faith and beliefs that are important. If you are a Witch at heart, it doesn't matter if that heart resides in the country or the city.

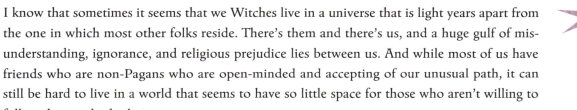

I know that sometimes it seems that we Witches live in a universe that is light years apart from the one in which most other folks reside. There's them and there's us, and a huge gulf of misunderstanding, ignorance, and religious prejudice lies between us. And while most of us have friends who are non-Pagans who are open-minded and accepting of our unusual path, it can still be hard to live in a world that seems to have so little space for those who aren't willing to follow the standard religions.

I think that we need to do something to change this.

Yes, it seems like an impossibly large task, but we're *Witches,* for goddess's sake—we know that nothing is impossible if you *will* it enough.

So where do we start?

By trying to focus not on those things that make us different (fun though they are sometimes) but rather on what we have in common.

If you look at the core beliefs of most religions—including Paganism—most of them start to sound kind of familiar. "Do unto others as you would have them do unto you" is not that different from "An it harm none, do as ye will." The threefold law of return is much the same as the Buddhist idea of karma. Most religions have rules (commandments) that forbid lying, just as the Witch's Rede of Chivalry bids us to be true to our word.

We may worship goddess and god in forms that are unfamiliar and uncomfortable to our neighbors, but most Witches believe that in essence our gods and their god are the same. My friend Nancy B. expressed this in a way that really rang true to me when she said, "I believe that god comes to all of us in the form that we can best understand and be most comfortable with, so that we can all worship in a fulfilling and meaningful way."

Now that's the kind of god that I can believe in—a loving god that comes to each of us and gives us the gift of connection with deity that suits us best.

So where does that leave us? Even if we can come to see that we have many of the same beliefs and values as the mundanes who surround us, how can we convince them of this important fact?

In perfect love and perfect trust.

No, this doesn't mean that you have to turn your back on that guy standing on your lawn with the burning cross; by all means, call the cops and run for the fire extinguisher.

What it does mean is that we have to find a way to accept them if we want them to accept us. And the way to do that is to love all those wonderful mundane folks with whom we share this planet and this universe, no matter how many obvious differences may lie between us. Love them even if they can't, right at this moment, love us.

So here's my theory about how we Witches go about making a place for ourselves in the world. We do the obvious stuff, like spreading awareness and working toward removing the ignorance that leads to fear that leads to hate. And while we are waiting for these things to happen (and thanking the goddess for the popularity of books like the Harry Potter series, which may result in an entire generation growing up thinking that Witches are cool, not evil), we do one other thing: we love them all.

Not just the nice ones who are our friends. Not just the indifferent ones who don't care about us one way or the other. Those are easy. We love the ones who fear us. We love the ones who hate us. For every negative thought or feeling that is sent in our direction, we return love, love, and more love.

As Witches, we know that if you meet negativity with negativity, it only makes it stronger. Our anger and fear only feed their anger and fear. But love is stronger than hate. I learned long ago (the hard way, as usual) that if someone sends negative energy in your direction, the strongest wall cannot keep it out. Defensive magick doesn't always work in the face of so much nastiness. What does work, every single time, is love. If you send love out, in the end, you will get love back.

Because love is truly universal. We all, at our core, want to be loved—*need* to be loved. So, as the Christians say, "Love thy neighbor," and remember that, in the end, we are all human beings sharing the same universe, the same planet, and the same deity who loves us all equally. Send out love into the universe, and you may be amazed by what comes back in return.

Quintessential Quotes: "Universe"

The universe is a dance of energy, a uni-verse, a single song of ever-changing rhythms and harmonies. Sustaining the melody of the physical world is a rich interplay of counterpoint and descant. We only see a fraction of the band of radiation that makes up the spectrum; we only hear a small range of the possible frequencies of sound. Ordinarily, we are conscious of only one isolated melody; we listen to only the piccolo out of an infinite orchestra. To trance is to shift and expand our awareness: to pick out the beat of the drum, the throbbing violins, the cry of the saxophones, to know the interwoven harmonies played in new keys, to thrill to the souring symphony itself.
—Starhawk, *The Spiral Dance*

Ask Magic the Cat:
"Unlucky"

Dear Magic the Cat,

    I am a very handsome cat who happens to be black (with stunning green eyes, in case you're interested). I have lived happily with my Witch for two years, but now she has a new mate who wants her to get rid of me because he thinks that black cats are unlucky. Should I worry?

    Black Bart in Bethesda

Dear Black Bart,

    As it happens, I am a black cat too, and I can tell you without question that we are anything but unlucky. In fact, it is well known that black cats make purrfect familiars. And I'm sure your Witch knows that. If she has had you for two years, and the dude is new, I can assure you that she is a lot more likely to get rid of him than she is to get rid of you. If necessary, you can encourage this by quietly whispering into her ear while she sleeps (as all familiars do). He'll be gone before you know it, and she'll be feeding you canned food for weeks to make up for all the mean things he said.

    Familiarly,
    Magic the Cat

    PS—You sound cute! If you ever get to upstate New York, look me up.

vervain

vacations

VERVAIN

Vervain (*Verbena officinalis*) is a VERY magickal plant. In fact, its folk names of enchanter's plant and simpler's joy attest to a long history of use by Witches, herbalists, and a variety of other magickal folks.

Vervain was sacred to Isis, and the Persians, Anglo-Saxons, and Romans used it to decorate altars dedicated to Venus and Jupiter. The Druids were said to have gathered it at night during a dark moon and then to have used it for divination. European colonists brought it with them to the New World where it now grows wild, waiting for the next generation of Witches to make use of it.

The plant itself is spiky in form and decorated with purplish-blue flowers. It is a member of the mint family, which means that it is easy to grow (and, in fact, will probably spread where you don't want it if you are not careful). It is traditionally harvested at Midsummer when the plant reaches its peak of height (about five feet) and power.

Vervain's long association with Witches and magick begins to make sense when you look at its list of magickal uses: love, purification, protection, luck, health, prosperity, divination, and (wait for it) aphrodisiacs. Specifically, vervain is used to change bad luck into good luck (who couldn't use that!) and turn enemies into friends. According to *The Element Encyclopedia of Witchcraft*, "No other plant is believed to have as much affection for people as does vervain ... a powerful and vigilant protector that may be used to smash hexes and reverse malevolent charms."[12]

Sally Dubats, in her wonderful book *Natural Magick: The Essential Witch's Grimoire*, says that vervain is "helpful for creating a soothing inner self" especially when mixed with chamomile and valerian, and recommends using a bundle of dried vervain as a smudge stick to clear the home of unwanted negativity.[13] (As opposed, I guess, to the kind you *do* want.)

---

12 Illes, 182.
13 Dubats, 131.

I like vervain both for its magickal usefulness and for its strong historical association with the very best aspects of magick, the Craft, and women's wisdom. Also, it is just damned pretty, which is a bonus. I plan to grow it in my garden this year and harvest it in time to use on our Midsummer altar, in honor of the goddess who so generously gifted us with such a wonderful herb. Thank you, lady of the growing things, mother of us all!

Vacations

We talk a lot about how to integrate our magickal lives with our mundane ones—not always an easy task in our hectic and often over-full existence. One way to do this is to take a vacation that somehow ties into your interests and experiences as a Witch.

Some people take a trip to Salem, Massachusetts, which has become something of a Mecca for those of the witchy persuasion. Others go to Europe and visit Stonehenge or other ancient magickal sites. There are even such places here in the good ol' US of A if you search them out, including one near Salem itself.

My group, Blue Moon Circle, has our own way of taking a magickal vacation: every summer we take a three-day weekend, pack up the husbands and the kids (those of us who have them), and go to a Renaissance fair.

This serves a couple of purposes. First and foremost, it is just plain fun. But more than just being fun, this vacation every year is an opportunity for us to bond as a magickal "family" and to get to know each other better outside the ritual setting. The guys get to hang out together (and make fun of us, no doubt) and become more comfortable with the strange, witchy women that their wives spend so much time cavorting with. (Sorry, Andrew: no, *not* naked.)

You can take a vacation that gets you back to nature somehow: go to the Grand Canyon and marvel in the power of the elements or go camping or to a beach. Or you can go to a Pagan festival, dedicated to all things Us. Most Pagan festivals are intended to be educational as well as entertaining, and feature workshops, lectures, demonstrations, and visits by Pagan authors. You may meet folks from many different traditions, attend rituals, and shop at vendors who specialize in Wiccan wares.

Either way, try to take a vacation that is in some way restful (sorry, people, Disney may be a hoot, but in no way is it restful) and that reconnects you to the people and powers that are important to you. And don't forget to have fun!

Quintessential Quotes:
"Village Witch"

The village witch, hedge witch, cottage witch, and even the kitchen witch are all direct descendants of the green practice of Witchcraft—the Old Religion. It can be considered irrelevant when some twentieth-century coven boasts of a chain of initiations back to Gardner if you consider that there have been and still are practicing Witches all over the world who have never heard of Gardner, much less care about any initiation he might want to bestow.

—Ann Moura, *Green Witchcraft*

Great Gods!
"Venus"

Venus is the Roman name for the Greek goddess Aphrodite, and both were (and are) considered to be goddesses of love and sex. But this image of the goddess didn't originate with the Greeks either. There are ties to Ishtar (Mesopotamia), Inanna (Sumeria), Astarte (Syria), and Hathor (Egypt), all of whom were some variation on the love/fertility/sex goddess...long may she rock!

Helpful Hints:
"Votive Variations"

Witches burn a lot of candles. They are a great tool and can be both beautiful and fun...but it can get a bit expensive. You don't necessarily need to buy fancy candles in the shape of the goddess or even "magickal" candles that have been preconsecrated for magickal use. Save those for the special occasions.

For everyday magick, you can use votives. These are small candles that can be found in any dollar store. They come in a variety of colors and tend to be fairly inexpensive. The white ones are a handy, all-purpose substitute if you don't have a particular color around. If you buy them from a Pagan store or catalog, you can even find votives that already contain the essential oils you'd want for doing magick anyway. And if you buy them in bulk, then you'll always have the candle you need for that last-minute spell.

Witch

wine

wisdom

Wiccan Rede

Wheel of the Year

W

WITCH

I talk a lot about the various aspects of being a Witch, but what exactly is a Witch, and how do you know if you are one?

Wicca is an ever-changing and evolving religion that prides itself on being open, accepting, and flexible. It can be different for each Witch that practices it, depending on her or his differing needs and desires, while still adhering to some basic tenets that we all share. So whether you call it Wicca or simply Witchcraft, if you believe in the following things, you are probably a Witch:

- A dualistic deity—that is to say, goddess and god (sometimes this is called pantheism, which is the worship of all gods).

- That the divine exists in everything, including plants, animals, and us (there is no true separation between the divine within and the divine without).

- The cyclical nature of the world, including the changing seasons (the Wheel of the Year) and the cycle of birth, life, death, and rebirth (reincarnation).

- Personal responsibility, or what you put out comes back to you (many but not all Witches specifically believe in the threefold law, which states that what you put out into the world comes back to you times three).

- That our words, thoughts, and actions have the power to affect change in the universe; the harnessing of those things in a purposeful way can be called magick and used to bring about positive change.

- All Witches can act as priests and priestesses and communicate directly with the divine.

- And perhaps most importantly, the Wiccan Rede (rule) of "An it harm none, do as ye will."

There is no such thing as the Wicked Witch, as far as I am concerned. If you willingly do harm (practice what some might call "black magick," although using black as a negative is not a witchy concept either), then you are not a Witch.

Witches, above all, try their best to be a positive force in the world.

So if those things sound like what you believe, and you think you are a Witch … you probably are! (Feel free to jump up and down for joy, kiss your cat, or run out and buy a new broom. Pointy black hat optional.)

WINE

At the end of most rituals, whether Solitary or celebrated with others, most Witches enact a part of the rite called either cakes and ale or cakes and wine. This involves eating a bite or two of something (usually bread, cookies, or cake, although it might be a piece of fruit) and drinking from a chalice (either wine, juice, or water). A blessing is said over each first and thanks given to the god/goddess for the gift.

Wine has a long history of association with the gods and celebration (for obvious reasons). I'm pretty sure that the first primitive human who stumbled across a batch of fermented grapes, tasted their delicious sweetness, and got a little buzz on yelled up to the heavens, "Thank you, Goddess!"

We've been doing variations on that ever since.

Many civilizations had at least one god who was specifically in charge of wine, Bacchus and Dionysus being two of the better-known ones. Bacchus even had a Roman festival named after him, the Bacchanalia—a whole day devoted to drinking, sex, and celebration (you know there were Witches at that one). Acan was a Mayan god of wine who specialized in a drink called *balche* made from fermented honey and the bark of a tree (um … yummy). And then we have the Hindu goddess Sura, who was said to have three eyes, a truly grotesque appearance, and no consort. Let this be a warning to you, girls...there is such a thing as *too much* wine.

In ancient Mesopotamia, date wine was considered a sacred food. (Personally, I like a good wine date, too. Oh, wait, that's something else.) Wine has been made from everything from dandelions to rice (sake) and most kinds of fruit. Mead, which is a kind of wine made from honey, is a particular favorite of Witches.

When used in ritual, wine symbolizes the gifts of the earth as well as the sweetness of the goddess's love. If you want, you can even make some at home with a little care and patience. So raise your chalice to the gods and sip (not gulp) the sweet nectar that is their gift to us.

Just remember that "harm none" means never drinking and driving, treating both wine and the gods with respect. (It is generally considered very poor manners to drink before a ritual, and it is impossible to work effective magick while drunk or drugged out.) It's best not to drink in any way that would cause harm to you or to others.

Like the other gifts that the gods give us, it is up to us to use it with wisdom, gratitude...and maybe a bit of cake.

Ask Onyx:
"Wine Wisdom"

Dear Onyx,

My coven likes to have wine in the chalice for cakes and ale at our rituals, but we recently had a problem at one of our open sabbats when it turns out that a guest had alcohol issues we didn't know about. Should we stop using wine and use something else?

Worried Witch in Wichita

Dear Worried,

This can be a real quandary for any Witches who celebrate in a group. You can deal with it in a couple of different ways. First of all, when it is just your coven, by all means use wine in the chalice if no one objects. For open rituals, if you don't know everyone who is coming well enough to be sure, or if there will be children present whose parents object to them having a sip of wine, you can either use juice instead of wine or take the trouble to talk to everyone ahead of time to make sure that there are no issues that you need to know about. Folks always have the option of just passing the cup, too. But if you want to include everyone, or if you are worried about exposing an alcoholic to temptation, then by all means just use cider or pomegranate juice—I assure you that the gods won't mind.

Bright blessings,
Onyx

WISDOM

One of my favorite bumper stickers is the one that says "Knowledge is power." And certainly having a lot of knowledge is likely to help you out in most circumstances of your daily life. But more important than knowledge, I think, is wisdom.

What's the difference, you ask?

Knowledge is knowing what to do, but wisdom is knowing whether or not it is a good idea to do it.

For example, you may have the knowledge of how to do a love spell to make that gorgeous guy next door go out with you. You know which candles to use, what herbs to burn, and what night of the week will make the spell the most powerful. On the other hand, if you have acquired any wisdom in your time as a Witch (and I hope you have), you will also know that making someone go out with you is not only against the rules of free will but also a just plain bad idea that is likely to come back and bite you in the butt.

So even though you have the knowledge that will allow you to do the spell, you have the wisdom to know not to do it anyway. (Just bake him some cookies, for goodness sake, or offer to fix his car—whatever you're good at.)

One of our primary goals as Witches is to become wiser. The very name of our craft is said to mean "wise" or "learned" (although there are many who say that isn't true, I like the concept anyway!) and much of our practice is aimed at increasing both our store of knowledge and the wisdom to use it well.

This is more than just a matter of studying hard (that's knowledge, not wisdom); it's a question of paying attention to the lessons that life and the gods send us and learning from our mistakes. For better or worse, the gods will keep sending you the same lessons over and over until you have learned whatever it is you are supposed to have learned.

The good news is that once you have finally achieved wisdom in that particular area (love or money or whatever it is), you will be able to stop banging your head against that particular wall. The bad news is that there is always another lesson…

Actually, if you're a Witch, that's good news, too. Because no matter how difficult the process of acquiring wisdom sometimes is, the path of the wise is the one that we as Witches have chosen. We choose to pay attention, to listen to our intuition, and to actively seek wisdom from Witches who are older or more experienced than us and from the gods themselves.

For it is only in this way that we can become the best people, and the best Witches, that we have the potential to be—and to then pass on whatever wisdom we manage to collect in this lifetime to the Witches who follow in our footsteps. And this, as much as anything else, is what it means to be a Witch.

WICCAN REDE

The Wiccan Rede (pronounced *reed*, it is an old word for "law") is the main tenet of Wicca. You could call it the Witches' golden rule. In its simplest form, it says, "An it harm none, do as ye will." There are a number of versions, varying in length, but these eight words lie at the core of all of them.

This "rule" is at the very heart of what it means to be a Witch. I know many Witches who do not consider themselves to be Wiccan (see my rant on Unity for more on that discussion), but they all follow the Wiccan Rede nonetheless. Witches, by definition, do not harm. Period. If you are purposely doing harm, you're not one of us, and there's another name for you. (Several, actually, none of them nice.)

This is not to say that Witches don't occasionally screw up, just like everybody else. (Well, not me, of course. And not you. Those *other* Witches…) But we do our best not to cause harm on purpose, and if we cause it by accident, we do what we can to fix it.

And in case you were thinking this sounds simple, keep in mind that "harm none" includes yourself. That's right: you're not supposed to be doing anything that is harmful to yourself, either. Thank the goddess that none of us ever smokes, drinks too much, stays up too late, or eats at McDonalds. (Oh, wait...)

The point is this: as Witches, we all do our best to follow the Wiccan Rede. And if, occasionally, we fall down in our attempts, we pick ourselves up, brush ourselves off, and get right back on the broomstick to try a little harder.

Here is the longer version of the Wiccan Rede that my group often recites together at the end of ritual:

> *Bide the Wiccan law ye must*
> *In perfect love and perfect trust*
> *Eight words the Wiccan Rede fulfill*
> *An it harm none, do as ye will*
> *Lest in thy self-defense it be*
> *Ever mind the Law of Three*
> *Follow this with mind and heart*
> *And merry ye meet, and merry ye part*
> *And merry meet again...*

Required Reading:
"Wicca: A Guide for the Solitary Practitioner"

Scott Cunningham may be one of the most prolific writers of books on Wicca and Witchcraft there is. Everything he has written is worth reading, too. But he is probably best known for his "beginner" book, *Wicca: A Guide for the Solitary Practitioner*. This is another book for every Witch, everywhere.

Witch 101:
"Witches' Rede of Chivalry"

The Witches' Rede of Chivalry can be found in Ed Fitch's book *Magical Rites from the Crystal Well*, containing work published in a popular Pagan magazine in the 1960s and '70s. *The Crystal Well* featured writing based primarily on Central and Eastern European magickal traditions.

The Witches' Rede of Chivalry may be written in somewhat archaic language, but it covers a number of important points, and I think it is worth taking a peek at. Here's an example to show you what I mean: "A Witch's word must have the validity of a signed and witnessed oath. Thus, give thy word sparingly, but adhere to it like iron."[14] Can't argue with that, can you?

---

14 Fitch, *Magical Rites*, 2.

WHEEL OF THE YEAR

The Wheel of the Year is the cycle of seasonal change, and it symbolizes the continuous larger cycle of birth, growth, death, and rebirth that all things must follow. The eight sabbats, or Pagan holidays, are like eight spokes on the wheel and mark the transitions from one season to another. The Wheel of the Year also honors the goddess and the god as they, too, follow the yearly sequence of growth and decay.

For instance, the Spring Equinox (Ostara) falls on the day when there is an equal amount of light and dark, and it signifies the return of increasing daylight and the beginning of the growing season. During this time on the wheel, the goddess is a maiden, full of youthful energy. The sun god, who was reborn at Yule, is a growing boy. By Beltane, the next spoke on the wheel, the god will have become a virile young man, ready to join with his consort the goddess in a great celebration of the fertility of summer.

The Wheel of the Year follows the triple goddess through her incarnations as maiden, mother, and crone. The god is born, grows strong, becomes the consort of the goddess, and then sacrifices himself, only to be reborn again.

This never-ending cycle, based on an agricultural year, still has meaning for modern Witches. It helps us reconnect to the earth and reminds us that we are only a small part of a much larger sequence of events that is played out over and over across the world. Each of us is born, will grow, and die. This is all a part of the Wheel of the Year. But never forget that hope is an intrinsic facet of the glory that is the wheel, and that when the wheel turns around in time, we too may return to follow the cycle yet again.

In the Witch's Tool Chest:
"Wave a Magick Wand"

A wand is another tool that is used to store and direct energy when doing magick. Usually made of wood, wands can be quite elaborate and incorporate crystals, symbols, and other magickal doodads. They can also be as simple as a small branch that fell off the willow tree in your backyard.

Like other magickal tools, wands should be cleansed and consecrated before their first use, then kept either on your altar or wherever else you store your magickal equipment. Sadly, I have never seen one that actually shoots sparks like Harry Potter's wand … but on the other hand, considering Witches and fire, maybe that's a good thing.

For woods that make good wands, see the entry on trees.

X

Xorguineria

X

X marks the spot. It is also the symbol for Gifu, one of my favorite runes.

Gifu is one of the Nordic runes, the kind that are probably used most often by Witches for divination and as magickal symbols. Gifu means "gift" and is always positive. (Some runes can have negative connotations when used in readings, but not this one. That is, in part, why I like it. Nobody likes to be the bearer of bad news, after all.)

Gifu usually has to do with partnership in some way, whether it is in business or love. If this rune shows up in a reading, it can indicate the beginning of a new romantic relationship or even marriage. I have often wondered if this is not the origin of the use of multiple Xs to signify kisses at the bottom of a letter.

Gifu can also stand for an actual gift, as in something that someone in your life will soon be giving you, or some kind of help for a troubling situation. Whenever I do magickal work for prosperity, I add Gifu to the symbols I inscribe onto the candle I use, to show that I am open to prosperity coming in the form of an unexpected gift.

I particularly like what Ralph Blum says about this rune (which he calls Gebu) in *The Book of Runes*: "Thus Gebu, the rune of partnership, has no Reverse because it signifies the gift of freedom from which flow all other gifts."[15]

And my favorite rune book, by Lisa Peschel, tells us why anyone would be happy to have this rune turn up in a reading: "Often this rune will appear when there is about to be relief from your troubles, and it usually betokens a time of peace and contentment in your life."[16]

X can mark *that* spot for me anytime.

---

15 Blum, 71.
16 Peschel, *A Practical Guide to the Runes*, 53.

Magic the Cat's Simple Spells:
"X Is for Excellent"

Here is some simple magick you can do with runes. Take a rune stone—for instance, Gifu—and hold it in your hands. (If you don't have a set of stones, just draw a picture of the stone you want to use. In the case of Gifu, a simple *X* will do.) Visualize its qualities. If you are using Gifu, you may want to focus on getting an unexpected gift, something that will bring you happiness. Then light a candle, and send your rune stone wish out into the universe.

XORGUINERIA

Xorguineria is a form of Witchcraft that was historically practiced in the Basque region. It was based primarily on "women's mysteries" (these are the so-called women's arts like weaving, sewing, and needlework that often played an important part in women's practice of the Craft for the simple reason that men never paid very much attention to them). Spinning was a particularly important focus of Xorguineria, and the Witch—or Xorguina—was said to spin spells in the moonlight while sitting at a crossroads.

Xorguineria apparently originated with the worship of the Witch goddess Mari, who bears an interesting resemblance to some aspects of another goddess who was also referred to by Mari's title of Queen of the Witches, Hecate.

Mari is still worshipped in the Basque area, despite the fact that after the Inquisition her followers, the Xorguina, were publicly labeled as Witches.

Mari is a mountain goddess, as befits the deity of such a mountainous land. She supposedly lives in a cave deep in the earth surrounded by precious stone and is pictured with the full moon behind her head, riding on a lightning bolt instead of a broom. (Let's see you do *that*, Harry Potter.)

Yule

yarrow

Yule

Yule is another name for the Winter Solstice, which falls every year on or around December 21. Yule is the longest night of the year, and it marks the point on the Wheel of the Year when the goddess gives birth to her son, the infant sun god.

It is a time of great rejoicing and merriment and is often observed with family and friends. Pagans bring in evergreen trees and boughs to symbolize life in the midst of the death of winter and exchange gifts to celebrate the holiday. They often sing traditional songs and feast on the hearty foods that will sustain them through the cold months ahead. Sometimes they hang up holly or mistletoe, which was sacred to the Druids.

Is any of this starting to sound strangely familiar?

If so, there is a good reason: the holiday currently known as Christmas was taken in great part from the Pagan traditions of Yule. Even the colors, green and red, were taken from the colors of the berries and evergreens that early Pagans used to decorate their homes, and if you listen to Christmas carols you will hear the words Yuletide or Yule pop up from time to time.

There is even a theory that the origins of Santa Claus can be traced back to the Oak King, who regains his throne at Yule from his counterpart the Holly King, who reigns from midsummer until midwinter. And that star on the top of the Christmas tree? Yup, you got it—that comes from the Witch's five-pointed star that symbolizes the five elements.

So why did the Christians take so many Pagan traditions and adopt them for their own? Historians theorize that when the Christians moved into Europe, they tried to force the Pagans who already lived there to change their beliefs and practices to Christian ones. When that didn't work (stubborn folk, us Pagans), they simply put a Christian twist to the holidays that were already celebrated in the region and called them their own. Pretty clever, when you think about it!

Yule was, at least in those days, a pretty raucous holiday, involving a great deal of drinking, carousing, and dancing in the streets from home to home (the origins of caroling, by the way)—so much so that the Pilgrims made Christmas illegal for a while once they moved here. (Big party poopers, those Pilgrims.)

Yule is a little calmer these days, but it is still a time for celebration and joy. And one of the benefits of having so many traditions in common with those observed by our Christian friends is that we can use the Winter Solstice as an opportunity to merge our two worlds in shared gratitude and appreciation for the light of friendship and family on the darkest day of the year.

Food of the Gods:
"Yule Wassail"

Wassail comes from a toast that translates as "be in good health" and can be made with alcohol (traditional) or without alcohol. It is usually made for Yule but can be served at any of the harvest festival holidays.

Combine a gallon of apple cider, a bottle of red wine, and a bunch of spices (usually in whole form, such as allspice berries, cinnamon sticks, cloves, and a slice or two of ginger) with maple syrup to sweeten (how much you use will depend on personal taste). Warm on the stovetop or in a Crock-Pot, then top with slices of orange or an apple sliced crosswise to show its pentacle shape. Then shout "Wassail!" and share with those you love.

YARROW

Another seriously witchy herb is yarrow (*Achillea millefolium*), also known as seven year's love, knight's milfoil, field hops, and ladies' mantle, among other things. Like vervain, yarrow is an herb that has a long association with the magickal arts.

As you might guess from its folk name seven year's love, yarrow is often used in love magick. Specifically, it has often been used in love sachets and magick that concerns marriage, as it is believed to have the power to keep a couple happy and together for seven years. (After that, I guess you're on your own!)

Yarrow is also used to boost psychic abilities and aid in divination (including love divination, as you might expect). It is said to be especially effective when used for clairvoyance.

The herb is also known for its ability to dispel negativity and banish unpleasant spirits and so was traditionally used for exorcism, as well as protection magick. A bundle of yarrow that is hung up in a house on Midsummer's Eve is supposed to protect all the inhabitants of that house from illness for a year to come. (And if it doesn't work, you can just eat a lot of garlic, my favorite herb.)

Like vervain, yarrow is also a beautiful plant that will grow easily in most Witches' gardens. In many parts of the country it can even be found growing wild in meadows or by the side of the road.

One small word of caution: as with all other herbs, be careful if taking this internally. It has been known to occasionally cause allergic reactions. (I once picked a bunch to make tea with, only to end up with quarter-sized blisters all over my hands—needless to say, I did not drink the tea…) So if you are prone to such things, approach all herbs carefully. If this is an issue, just use the herb in a charm, sachet, or amulet, or substitute a different herb that has the same properties. Luckily, there are many herbs that can be used for magickal work, and eventually each Witch finds the ones that suit him or her best.

Witch 101:
"Year and a Day"

You will often find a reference to "a year and a day" in books about Witch-craft. This time period is traditional for everything from a short-term handfast-ing to the duration of study required for many of the coven systems that use degrees. It doesn't always have to be taken literally (my additional period of study before becoming a high priestess was about a year and three months, just because that's how long it took), but it is a good rule of thumb for anything that needs to be undertaken slowly and with considerable thought and effort.

zodiac

zenith

ZODIAC

Sit around in any bar for long enough and someone is sure to come up and ask you what your sign is. (I always say, "Go slow, dangerous curves"—but that's another story.)

They are talking about zodiac signs, an important component in astrology, an ancient science used by Witches (and a lot of other people) for divination and magick.

The Encyclopedia of Magic and Alchemy by Rosemary Ellen Guiley defines astrology as an ancient system "based on a principle attributed to Hermes Trismegistus: 'as above, so below.'"[17] Hmm...isn't *that* interesting?

Astrology uses the positions of the planets and the stars to predict the future and explain the past. Zodiac signs in particular are often used to shed light on the various character traits that people tend to have and can be used as a tool for self-exploration and self-improvement.

Zodiac signs and astrology are used in casting horoscopes as well. Using the date and time of your birth (*horoscope* is Greek for "I look at the hour"), an astrologer can come up with predictions on future trends or events in your life. Astrology has been practiced by cultures around the world throughout history, including the Chinese, Mayans, Egyptians, and Greeks. During the Renaissance, it was considered to be a serious science but then dropped out of favor until relatively recently.

Witches don't just use zodiac signs to find out if that cute person they met in the bar is a good match. Astrology can also be used to determine the best time to do a spell or a ritual. The signs of the zodiac are divided into earth, air, fire, and water, just like many of the other elements of Witchcraft, which may help you decide which time is best for doing any particular magickal work.

If, for instance, you want to work on magick for prosperity, you may wish to do a spell when the moon is in Taurus, Virgo, or Capricorn—all earth signs. On the other hand, if you want to do magick for something emotional (like love), then you may decide to wait until the moon is in Cancer, Scorpio, or Pisces, since they are all water signs.

---

17 Guiley, 8.

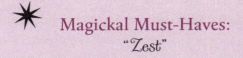

Magickal Must-Haves:
"Zest"

There is one ingredient necessary for Witchcraft that cannot be bought in any Pagan store or grown in any garden. That ingredient is zest. Webster's defines zest as "keen enjoyment, relish, gusto." I define it as that "extra something" that each Witch brings to his or her practice; that spark of divinity that passes from the gods through us and back out into the universe. It is this zest that powers our spells, drives us to learn, and draws us to each other. Whatever other tools or ingredients you bring to your magic, don't forget to bring your sense of enjoyment, relish, and gusto. Then go for it!

Required Reading:
"Z. Budapest"

Z. (Zsuzsanna) Budapest was one of the architects of the early Wicca movement. A hereditary Witch from Hungary, Budapest wrote *The Holy Book of Women's Mysteries: Feminist Witchcraft, Goddess Rituals, Spellcasting and Other Womanly Arts*, a classic in the feminist and Dianic Witchcraft traditions. Noted also for her influence on other important Wiccan women such as Starhawk, who quotes her as once saying, "In our tradition, it's good to have needs and desires. We are not a religion of self-abnegation," Z. Budapest is still well worth reading today. (And having met her, I can also tell you that she is as charming and beautiful as she is wise.)

Zenith

Roget's Thesaurus gives the following words as synonyms for zenith: summit, pinnacle, top, peak, height, apex, acme, maximum, crown, culmination, and high point. These are all pretty good descriptions of what we as Witches are aiming for in our practice of magick and in our lives.

Not so much to be the best, as in "she's the best at algebra" or "he's the best baseball player," but rather best as in "the best Witch I can be" or "the best human being I can be."

We strive (most of us at least) to become more than we were born into this lifetime as being. To improve ourselves so that by the time we are done with this space of existence and ready to rest in the Summerlands for a while, we can look back on our lives and be satisfied that we will enter into our next lifetime as wiser, smarter, more loving human beings.

Do any of us ever reach our zenith, that high point where we can say that we are truly the best that we can be? Probably not. But the journey is as important as the destination, and as long as we continue to reach for the stars, we are following the path that the gods have laid out for us, and that is all they ask.

If this book has helped you in some small way to become a better Witch or a better person—if it has taught you anything about the Craft, given you any insight into yourself or other Witches, inspired or amused you—then my work here is done. (If not, I guess I will just have to get started on the next book and try to do better!)

I wish you love and laughter, growth and wisdom, adventure and serenity. May the goddess and the god watch over you as you walk the path toward your zenith, wherever that path may take you.

Blessed be.

—Deborah Blake (Onyx) &
(Magic the Cat)

Resources and Recommended Reading

Blake, Deborah. *Circle, Coven & Grove: A Year of Magickal Practice.* Woodbury, MN: Llewellyn, 2007.

Blum, Ralph. *The Book of Runes: A Handbook for the Use of an Ancient Oracle: The Viking Runes.* New York: St. Martin's Press, 1982.

Buckland, Raymond. *Buckland's Complete Book of Witchcraft.* St. Paul: Llewellyn, 2003.

———. *Wicca for Life: The Way of the Craft—from Birth to Summerland.* New York: Citadel Press, 2001.

Connor, Kerri. *The Pocket Spell Creator: Magickal References at Your Fingertips.* Franklin Lakes, NJ: New Page Books, 2003.

Cunningham, Scott. *Cunningham's Encyclopedia of Magical Herbs.* St. Paul: Llewellyn, 1985.

———. *The Complete Book of Incense, Oils & Brews.* St. Paul: Llewellyn, 1989.

———. *Cunningham's Encyclopedia of Crystal, Gem & Metal Magic.* St. Paul: Llewellyn, 1988.

———. *Cunningham's Encyclopedia of Wicca in the Kitchen.* St. Paul: Llewellyn, 1990.

———. *Living Wicca: A Further Guide for the Solitary Practitioner.* St. Paul: Llewellyn, 1993.

———. *Magical Herbalism.* St. Paul: Llewellyn, 1982.

———. *Wicca: A Guide for the Solitary Practitioner.* St. Paul: Llewellyn, 1988.

Digitalis, Raven. *Shadow Magick Compendium*. Woodbury, MN: Llewellyn, 2008.

Dubats, Sally. *Natural Magick: The Essential Witch's Grimoire*. New York: Kensington, 1999.

Dunwich, Gerina. *The Wicca Garden: A Modern Witch's Book of Magickal and Enchanted Herbs and Plants*. New York: Citadel Press, 1996.

Fitch, Ed. *Magical Rites from the Crystal Well: A Classic Text for Witches & Pagans*. St. Paul: Llewellyn, 1984.

Galenorn, Yasmine. *Embracing the Moon: A Witch's Guide to Ritual Spellcraft and Shadow Work*. St. Paul: Llewellyn, 1998.

Greer, John Michael. *The New Encyclopedia of the Occult*. St. Paul: Llewellyn, 2003.

Grimassi, Raven. *Encyclopedia of Wicca & Witchcraft*. St. Paul: Llewellyn, 2000.

Guiley, Rosemary Ellen. *The Encyclopedia of Magic and Alchemy*. New York: Checkmark Books, 2006.

———. *The Encyclopedia of Witches & Witchcraft: Second Edition*. New York: Checkmark Books, 1999.

Holland, Eileen. *The Wicca Handbook*. York Beach, ME: Samuel Weiser, 2000.

Illes, Judika. *The Element Encyclopedia of Witchcraft*. Hammersmith, UK: Harper Element, 2005.

Johnson, Cait. *Witch in the Kitchen: Magical Cooking for All Seasons*. Rochester, VT: Destiny Books, 2001.

Johnstone, Michael. *The Ultimate Encyclopedia of Spells*. New York: Gramercy Books, 2003.

Jordan, Michael. *Encyclopedia of Gods: Over 2,500 Deities of the World.* New York: Facts on File, Inc., 1993.

Merriam-Webster's Collegiate Dictionary: Eleventh Edition. Springfield, MA: Merriam-Webster Incorporated, 2007.

Morrison, Dorothy. *Everyday Moon Magic.* St. Paul: Llewellyn, 2003.

Moura, Ann. *Green Witchcraft: Folk Magic, Fairy Lore & Herb Craft.* St. Paul: Llewellyn, 1996.

Nahmad, Claire. *Catspells: A Collection of Enchantments for You and Your Feline Companion.* Philadelphia: Running Press, 1993.

Peschel, Lisa. *A Practical Guide to the Runes: Their Uses in Divination and Magick.* St. Paul: Llewellyn, 1990.

Starhawk. *The Spiral Dance: A Rebirth of the Ancient Religion of the Great Goddess.* New York: HarperCollins, 1979, 1989, 1999.

Telesco, Patricia. *Your Book of Shadows: How to Write Your Own Magickal Spells.* New York: Citadel Press, 1999.

Tuitean, Paul, and Estelle Daniels. *Pocket Guide to Wicca.* Freedom, CA: The Crossing Press, 1998.

Weinstein, Marion. *Positive Magic: Occult Self-Help.* New York: Earth Magic, 1994. First edition, New York: Simon & Schuster, 1978.

Wood, Gail. *Rituals of the Dark Moon: 13 Lunar Rites for a Magical Path.* St. Paul: Llewellyn, 2001.

Wood, Jamie, and Tara Seefeldt. *The Wicca Cookbook: Recipes, Ritual, and Lore.* Berkeley, CA: Celestial Arts, 2000.